Rushing Thru the Dark

Drama, Poetry, and Art

Autumn 2023

Choeofpleirn Press

Rushing Thru the Dark

Autumn 2023
Drama, Poetry, and Art

Copyright 2023

Choeofpleirn Press Editors
James P. Cooper, Poetry & Art
Ruth J. Heflin, Drama & Art

Choeofpleirn Press is a small, private press publishing literary journals in northeastern Kansas at the foot of the Glacial Hills. Our goal is to promote the best written and photographed creations we can in each magazine, with the eventual goal of publishing books.

We publish four separate journals a year: *Coneflower Café* (Spring), *Glacial Hills Review* (Summer), *Rushing Thru the Dark* (Autumn), and the *Best of Choeofpleirn Press* (Winter). The Spring, Summer, and Autumn journals are each dedicated to one of three major genres of storytelling: short fiction, nonfiction, and drama. The top three winners of the five creative contests held by CP—the Derick Burleson Poetry Prize, the Ben Nyberg Short Fiction Award, the Phil Heldrich Nonfiction Award, the Susan Hansell Drama Prize, and the Mary Cassatt Art Award—are republished in the Winter magazine. The first place award in each category comes with a cash prize.

CP also features a poem-of-the-week on our website, www.choeofpleirnpress.com.

Readers can purchase individual digital issues of each magazine directly through our website. Digital individual issues cost $6 each; annual digital subscriptions cost $24.

Readers who prefer print copies can purchase individual magazines from Amazon.

Writers can also purchase classified or photo ads to appear in specific magazines in an effort to promote their own works or websites. See our website for details.

Contact Choeofpleirn Press through choeofpleirnpress@gmail.com.

Cover photo: "Stratocumulus Sunsets" by Gerald Uyeno. The triptych, originally titled "Northwest Storm Front Approaches Ventura" #1, #2, and #3, was taken at Oxnard Beach, California.

ISSN (Online) 2769-0016 (Print) 2768-797X
ISBN (print) 979-8-9885631-5-0 (digital) 979-8-9885631-6-7

Editors' Note

For Ruth, the primary difference between reading a script and reading a short story comes from the fact that a script is mostly dialog (or monologue, as the case may be), so that the weight of human feeling or emotion is stronger in drama than it is in fiction.

Perhaps that emotional energy comes, in part, from the fact that characters on a stage or on screen are forced to communicate with each other, in order for the viewer to understand what they are thinking and feeling, something usually told to us through narrators in fiction.

Both fiction and drama, however, make viewers into "flies on the wall," to use a cliché favored by Ernest Hemingway. As a literary minimalist, Hemingway strove, like Gertrude Stein before him, to give readers no more than what they needed to figure out what was actually happening between two people in his short stories, such as his infamous short, short story, "Hills Like White Elephants."

While many real human beings might avoid revealing their truths to each other, even to people they love unconditionally, characters in plays and screenplays must bare their souls to us, The Watchers. In that way, they show us how we, too, could be better human beings, even when the characters in the dramas we love are not so nice themselves.

We hope you enjoy our dramatic selections in this issue of *Rushing Thru the Dark*. As is our tradition, we are giving away copies of the digital magazine to dramatic groups across the globe who are designated by our contributors. In this way, we hope to promote the excellent quality of drama being written today.

As observed by James Hatch, a former Navy Seal who recently obtained a bachelor's degree, literature is the "connective tissue" between human beings.[1]

Stories have long shaped our perceptions of what it means to be human, including influencing us to draw our tribes around us or to be more inclusive in our social spheres. Here's hoping these selections help us become more inclusive.

---

[1] Quoted in Erika Ryan's article "A Former Navy Seal Went to College at 52. His Insight Led to a New Class," for NPR, published on September 18, 2023.

Choeofpleirn Press Supporters

We wish to thank the following donors for their generous support of our press:

Christine Andersen

Karyn Bruce

Joseph Cappello

G.W. Clift

Jeffrey Feingold

Louise Kantro

Madeline Wise

and several donors who wish to remain anonymous.

Contents

Cid Andrenelli 206
Aline J. Awada 242
Alex Barr 5
Mark Blickley 129
David Blumenfeld 240
Stacey Bowerman 68, 69, 70
Steve Brisendine 108
William Robert Carey 180
Mark Clarke 4, 67, 71, 176, 179
Karen Colstrom 1, 34, 124, 128,154, 201, 231
Willy Conley 235
Bill Connolly 232, 233
Brian Daldorph 107
Suzanna C. de Baca 145, 146
Linda Enders 243
Andrew Graber 31, 106
Peter J. Grady 72
John Grey 125
Patricia L. Hamilton 126, 127
Susan Hansell 155
Rosalie Hendon 177, 178
Arnold Johnston 2, 3
Roberta I. Mayes 198, 234, 239,
Michael Moreth 110, 151, 205
Margaret Pearce 111
Jennifer M. Phillips 152, 153
Marge Piercy 32, 33
Judith Present 148
Kait Quinn 200, 202, 204
S.M. Stevens 35
Gerald Uyeno cover, 147
Buff Whitman-Bradley 109

A Winter's View

Karen Colstrom

Gatwick, 1998

Arnold Johnston

We landed at Gatwick in early June,
But England, unexpectedly, was hot.
The rental car would not appear 'til noon
The next day, so we settled on a spot
With air-conditioning at the hotel,
Soaked in the pool with dinner yet to come.
My father had to check in there as well,
But renting a cool room involved a sum
He balked at, so he found himself a place,
Cut-rate, with no a-c. The heat was less
Important than the price. It was the base,
Like his old barracks in the town, I guess,
From which he ventured forth to find
His favorite places, those he'd known so well
When he was stationed here. We didn't mind
The downtime on our own. We knew he'd tell
Us all about it in the restaurant.
He did, of course. He'd found his favorite pub,
The place the Territorials would haunt
For pints and all the standard English grub.
And what fond memories did his visit wake?
We waited patiently to hear the tale.
Would it involve old comrades, or the ache
Of lost romance that time could never stale?
But, unsurprisingly, what irked him still,
The memory preserved for all those years,
Was that some welcher stuck him with the bill
For everybody's whiskies, snacks, and beers.
The punchline to the dinner and the gab:
He aired his grievance; we picked up the tab.
Our lives were haunted by his memories;
We never stiffed him, never brought him ease.

Winter Dream

Arnold Johnston

Our son drives us along a snow-clogged track
And slides amid a blinding swirl of white.
The journey ends within a *cul-de-sac*
When the car strikes a sign that, like a kite,
Rises and tumbles before us. The snow
Is axle-deep. He goes for help the way
We came, while you start off, careful and slow,
Toward a stand of evergreens. I stay
Beside the car and read the makeshift sign,
Scrawled with the owner's blunt and misspelled plea
For drivers to respect his borderline.
I peer through the feathery swirl and see
You standing near a stunted evergreen
That shivers off its white shroud, letting go
A scarlet cardinal, his crest unseen
Beneath a tiny cap of dazzling snow.
The small bird trembles like a sacred heart.
And holding hands we watch as day grows late,
The wind blows cold; and hoping not to part,
We face the night together, and we wait.

Elevator

Mark Clarke

ARMOR

A one-act play
Running time 30 minutes

Alex Barr

SYNOPSIS
> Two people from different cultural backgrounds find social and familial connections through puppets built by one and bought by the other.

CHARACTERS
> AZRA DIMOGLU
> Age 23. Born of Turkish parents from Kayseri, lived in United Kingdom since she was two, now works in North London as a social worker. Unknown to Simon, she's married his estranged son.
>
> SIMON STANLEY
> Age 49. Former sculptor, art-college lecturer, and puppeteer in South London. Now lives alone and works as a blacksmith. Aims to sell his Sicilian-style puppets.

SETTING
> An ante-room in Simon's workshop in a disused South London factory. Furniture creates the scene: two battered armchairs and a portable workbench. On the floor are a kettle, a mug, remains of takeaways, and odd bits of steel. One entrance leads from outside, the other to the workshop. Towards the audience an imaginary window whose blind is remote-controlled. A battered trunk. From it during the action are taken three Sicilian-style puppets, three feet high. Saint George is in full armor, King Almidor in partial armor with brightly coloured baggy trousers. King Ptolemy need only be seen with his back to the audience (unless played in the round) which simplifies his construction.

TIME
> The present.

AT RISE
> (AZRA enters from outside, picks her way over bits of steel, peers into the workshop.)

AZRA

Hello?

SIMON
(Off stage)

Get back.

(Torch sound cut. SIMON comes from the workshop wearing grubby overalls and a welding mask. He removes the mask.)

                              SIMON (continued)
Don't you know not to come near a welding torch?

                              AZRA
Are you Simon Stanley?

                              SIMON
Yes. Who the hell are you?

                              AZRA
Azra Dimoglu. We spoke on the phone, remember. About the puppet show you advertised on eBay. I arranged to come today.

                              SIMON
                              (Searches)
Where's the bloody diary?

                              AZRA
Is that it?

                              SIMON
No, is it hell.

                              AZRA
That then.

                              SIMON
                              (Finding it)
You're not in here.

                              AZRA
You're on the wrong month.

        (SIMON finds the right entry.)

                              AZRA, Cont.
See? And you took some finding. Miles from the nearest Tube stop.

        (Pause)

What do you make with all this iron?

                              SIMON
Why do you ask?

        (AZRA shrugs.)

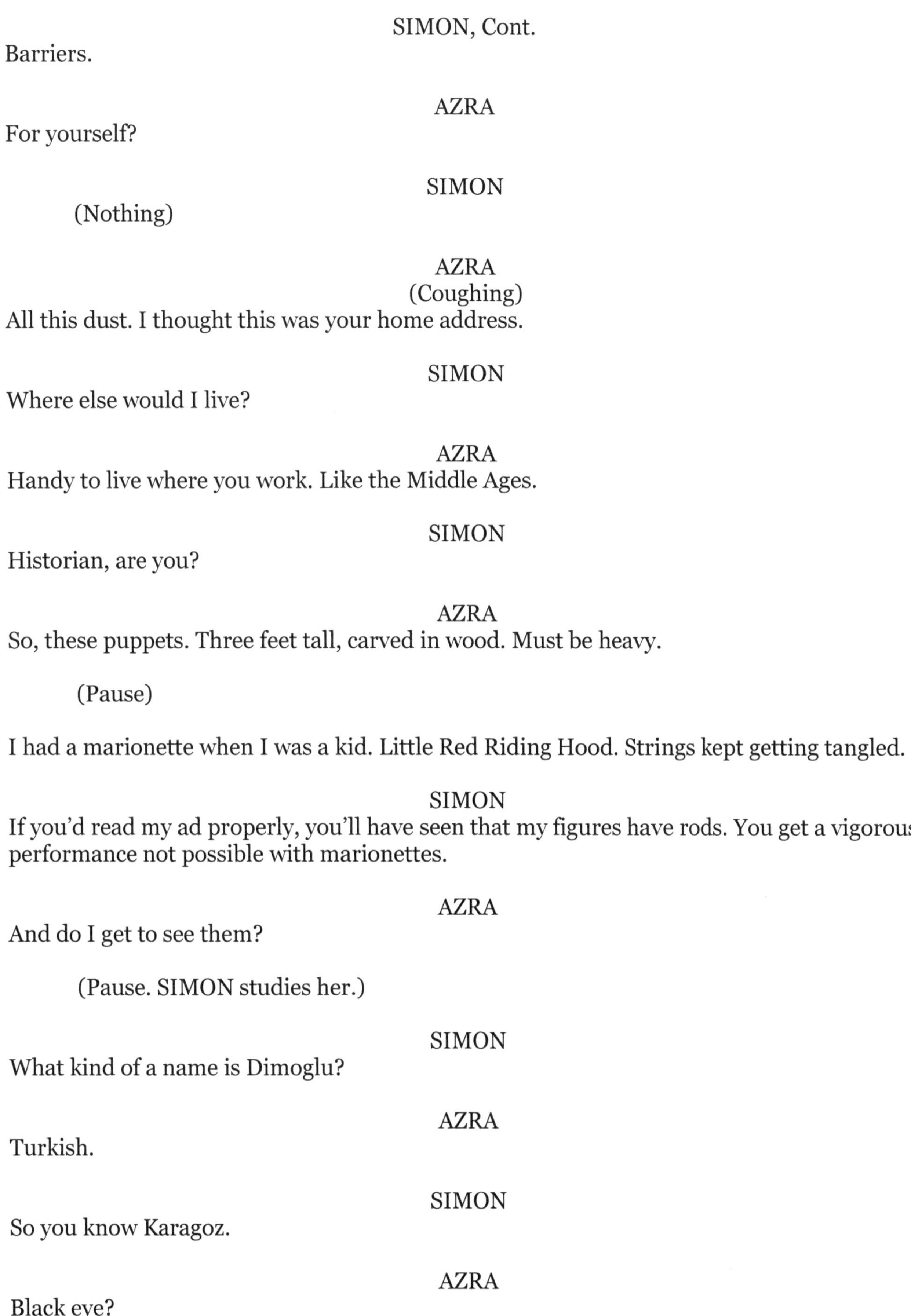

SIMON, Cont.

Barriers.

AZRA

For yourself?

SIMON

(Nothing)

AZRA
(Coughing)

All this dust. I thought this was your home address.

SIMON

Where else would I live?

AZRA

Handy to live where you work. Like the Middle Ages.

SIMON

Historian, are you?

AZRA

So, these puppets. Three feet tall, carved in wood. Must be heavy.

(Pause)

I had a marionette when I was a kid. Little Red Riding Hood. Strings kept getting tangled.

SIMON

If you'd read my ad properly, you'll have seen that my figures have rods. You get a vigorous performance not possible with marionettes.

AZRA

And do I get to see them?

(Pause. SIMON studies her.)

SIMON

What kind of a name is Dimoglu?

AZRA

Turkish.

SIMON

So you know Karagoz.

AZRA

Black eye?

7

                                    SIMON
The hero of the traditional Turkish shadow puppet play. The equivalent of Punch.

                                    AZRA
I've lived in Britain since I was two.

                                    SIMON
Never been back to Turkey?

                                    AZRA
Once when I was ten. Then when I was twenty.

                                    SIMON
But you never saw Karagoz.

                                    AZRA
Too busy catching up with family.

          (Pause)

Well?

          (From the trunk SIMON takes St George and King Almidor and holds them up.)

                                    SIMON
Press that remote.

          (AZRA finds a remote and presses the switch. The puppets are suddenly spotlit.)

                                    AZRA
Wow.

                                    SIMON
Saint George, Champion of Christendom. Almidor, King of Barbary.

                                    AZRA
I love how the light shows up the embossing on their shields and armor.

                                    SIMON
So you like the armor.

                                    AZRA
Must have taken a hell of a lot of work.

                                    SIMON
          (Laughs grimly)

                                    AZRA
Saint George has an interesting face. I've got a client with that expression.

                                        SIMON
A client? You an art dealer?

                                        AZRA
No.

        (Peers into the trunk)

Hey, who's this?

                                        SIMON
Don't lift her out. Her dress is fragile.

                                        AZRA
It's gorgeous. Did you make it?

                                        SIMON
No.

                                        AZRA
Who did?

                                        SIMON
Why do you want to know?

                                        AZRA
Sorry. Well? Who is this mystery woman?

                                        SIMON
The Princess Sabra. Daughter of King Ptolemy of Egypt.

                                        AZRA
Ah, the one George rescues from the dragon. She's beautiful.

                                        SIMON
That's the whole idea.

                                        AZRA
Right. So if she was ugly he'd leave her to die? When you made her you must have felt like
God making Eve. Who's the bug-eyed bloke next to her?

                                        SIMON
King Ptolemy of Egypt.

                                        AZRA
Oh, of course. Your photos on eBay weren't clear. He looks a bit of a plonker. Being
foreign, I suppose. And Sabra's mum?

                            SIMON

Not in the story.

                            AZRA

Now why doesn't that surprise me?

                            SIMON

Look, there's no point rooting around in the trunk. Make me an offer and I'll know you're serious. You can see the rest in here. I've got a feeling I'm wasting my time though.

        (Gives her a photo album from the trunk.)

                            AZRA

'The Seven Champions of Christendom.' Ha. Who do they fight?

                            SIMON

Saracens. Moors.

                            AZRA

Muslims in general. Oh wow, the dragon. Look at his wings. Does he breathe real fire? Is there a blowlamp?

        (He snatches the album from her.)

                            SIMON

A blowlamp on stage? What planet are you from? Insurance is a nightmare as it is. Who are these clients of yours?

                            AZRA

I'm a social worker.

                            SIMON

Oh Christ. You want my figures buggered about by junkies?

                            AZRA

I work in foster-care. I find families for children who—

                            SIMON

So what the hell are you doing here?

                            AZRA

I have a friend who's had experience with these…With puppets very like these.

                            SIMON

So why isn't she here?

                            AZRA

He. We decided I should come alone.

                              SIMON
It's not that bugger Williams.

                              AZRA
No.

                              SIMON
Cavendish? He's a waste of space.

                              AZRA
No.

                              SIMON
And there's just the two of you.

                              AZRA
There's another on the way.

                              SIMON
Where? Stuck on the motorway? Look, can we get this over with, I find this painful. Do you
want to make an offer or not? I want these out of my life.

                              AZRA
So you can go on welding barriers?

                              SIMON
This is a nightmare.

                              AZRA
You're right. Even drug addicts offer you a drink.

                              SIMON
There's water in the tap.

         (She looks at the mug with horror, takes a bottle of mineral water out of her bag,
         drinks.)

                              AZRA
I'd like to see a show.

                              SIMON
Oh my God.

                              AZRA
How else can I tell whether to make you an offer?

                              SIMON
There's an old DVD somewhere.

                                    AZRA
I'd like you and I to do a scene together.

                                    SIMON
You may be young and think you can charm your way into anything, but you'll get old like
everyone else.

        (Pause)

Oh come on then.

        (He clears a space, during:)

So where are you from again?

                                    AZRA
Milford Haven.

                                    SIMON
In Turkey.

                                    AZRA
Kayseri. In what used to be Cappadocia. Where Saint George is supposed to be from.

                                    SIMON
In my version, from the eighteenth century chapbook, he comes from Coventry.

                                    AZRA
Coventry?

        (Laughs, coughs)

                                    SIMON
        (Places the script on the portable bench)

You read Ptolemy. I'll read George. You're on. I enter.

        (as George)

Yield, King of Egypt! The Christian armies are victorious. All of your realm is under our
control.

                                    AZRA
        (as Ptolemy)

George of England! Am I a stranger to you? King Ptolemy, whose daughter you saved from
the dragon. I beg you to be merciful.

SIMON

Why should I spare your miserable life?

AZRA

I will do anything you desire.

SIMON

Vain words, King of Egypt. Your daughter is mine, your crown is mine by right after your death. What more can you perform?

AZRA

Noble George, I believe it is your nature to be generous. You would otherwise have killed me outright. This generosity must be a Christian quality. I therefore embrace your faith, together with all my people.

(Suppresses a laugh)

SIMON

Oh happy day for Christendom. Once more I embrace you as my friend.

(as himself)

They're supposed to embrace.

AZRA

(as herself)

I'm trying. Carry on.

SIMON

(as George)

I must bring this joyful news to my army. It will give them heart for the invasion of Persia.

AZRA
(Laughs)

Invasion of Persia...very topical.

SIMON

(as himself)

You haven't a clue, have you? I've never seen anything so wooden. This rod (to the head) gives positive control, this one (to the hand) subtle control of gesture.

AZRA

Give me a chance. Anyway, it's a rubbish part, King Ptolemy the wimp. This one's got more bottle.

(Takes out King Almidor)

13

SIMON

You can't do a fight scene.

AZRA

Is this string through his hand to draw the sword?

SIMON

Oh, all right. I'll get the music ready. I'm George. Here's your place in the script. Go.

AZRA

(as Almidor)

Who dares to speak thus to the King of Barbary? Ah! George of England.

SIMON

(as George)

Draw and defend, or yield yourself recreant.

AZRA

Son of a camel, I spit at you and defy you. Defend yourself.

(Music accompanies a rhythmic fight. After a while SMON breaks off and cuts the music.)

AZRA

(as herself)

Why have you stopped?

SIMON

(as himself)

It's a waste of time. You've no aptitude whatsoever. What do you propose to do with this if you do buy it?

AZRA

Ditch this script for a start. "The Christian armies are victorious." "All of Egypt shall become Christian." Loud cheers from the neo-cons.

SIMON

This tradition has a social function.

AZRA

Scare the shit out of Muslims?

SIMON

It allows the audience to deal with success and failure, the ups and downs of fortune.

                                    AZRA
And has it helped you come to terms with...

                                    SIMON
With what?

                                    AZRA
With life.

                                    SIMON
I'll ask you again, why are you here?

        (Pause)

You don't seem to know. These figures have a stiff dignity and authority appropriate to the legends they perform. I didn't spend years making them to have them move like invalids.

                                    AZRA
No? Well maybe while you were bashing away at armor in your cellar you should have thought about the political implications of these legends. Oh, but it's fashionable to take the piss out of Muslims nowadays. You're right, I don't know why I am here.

                                    SIMON
So if you think I wasted my time on this show stop bloody well wasting more of it. You can't even read a script convincingly. (Cockney accent) 'I'm the King of Egypt, innit?'

                                    AZRA
You bastard.

        (She goes out. SIMON replaces the puppets and turns off the spot. He stands for a
        moment, goes towards his workshop, stops as a thought strikes him.)

                                    SIMON
How the hell...?

        (He strides towards the outside entrance and cannons into AZRA coming back.)

                                SIMON, Cont.
Damn. Damn. Are you hurt?

                                    AZRA
No. Why were you coming after me?

                                    SIMON
Because I want to know something. How the hell did you know I worked on the armor in the cellar? Have you been spying on me?

                                    AZRA

An art college lecturer in South London—where else would you live but a big run-down
Victorian house with cellars?

                                   SIMON

How did you know I was an art college lecturer?

                                    AZRA

Maybe I looked you up online. Did you always work on the figures alone?

                                   SIMON

Sometimes...Kate, my daughter, helped.

                                    AZRA

Till she left.

                                   SIMON

How did you know that?

                                    AZRA

It's what daughters do.

                                   SIMON

She's in the States, studying something incomprehensible at MIT.

                                    AZRA

Yes.

                                   SIMON

What do you mean, 'yes'? Is that somehow inevitable?

                                    AZRA

Did anyone else help you in the cellar?

                                   SIMON

What?

                                    AZRA

You see, I know very little about you.

                                   SIMON

Good. (Pause) You were coming back. You forgot something?

                                    AZRA

Yes.

                                   SIMON

Where is it?

AZRA

All around. The smell of this place. I've been wondering why it makes me feel...I'm not giving up, right?

SIMON

You've lost me.

AZRA

This bitter greasy smell of steel bars. I suddenly remembered Turkey when I was ten. My granddad, the blacksmith, greeting me the first time he'd seen me for seven years. His hands on my face, rough, but kind. His eyes damp with tears. His face was lined and when he smiled the lines all changed and...

    (She breaks down)

SIMON

You'd better sit down.

AZRA

I know why I'm here.

SIMON

You were saying. About Turkey.

AZRA

Suddenly, for the first time, I had a family. In Milford there was only mum. Not exactly cheerful. Dad died when I was eight. Suddenly there were aunts and uncles and cousins and hugs and kisses and huge tables of bread and olives and baklava, and I wasn't just some weird kid who got sent away from her friends' houses for having the wrong God. My relatives, my family, made me feel as if they'd been waiting and waiting unsatisfied and now it was all right because I was there. Even though I didn't speak much Turkish I wasn't alone anymore. Do you know what it's like to be alone? Yes, of course, no-one else would share this mess. I was with people who gave support, who cared. Sorry, I was rude about the mess.

SIMON

It's fair enough. I've been rude to you. You got on my wick when you first arrived.

AZRA

But now you see my vulnerable side you can afford to like me.

SIMON

Bloody social workers. Thinking you can suss people out.

AZRA

Do you know any social workers apart from me?

    (Long pause)

AZRA, Cont'd

I think you do.

SIMON

I may have led a messy life, but thank Christ I've never needed a social worker.

AZRA

So you don't know one called Phil.

(Long pause)

No?

SIMON

Phil who?

AZRA

Phil Stanley, Mr Stanley.

(Long pause)

Well say something.

SIMON

You know my... You know him.

AZRA

We're— We're colleagues. Of a sort. He's in housing.

SIMON

Well, I didn't wish to know that, thank you, Miss Dimoglu. All I want to hear about is who's going to join you if you buy my puppet theatre, because on your own you've as much chance as a dog playing the organ.

AZRA

What if my partner in this venture, and my colleague Phil, are one and the same?

(Long pause)

Or don't you want to hear about the son you haven't seen for seven years?

SIMON

Six. Six. Can I make a suggestion? Get your backside off my chair and leave.

AZRA

I haven't finished inspecting the goods.

SIMON

Why should I show them to you?

                                    AZRA
You do a good line in sulking, don't you?

        (SIMON opens the trunk and turns the spot back on.)

                                 AZRA, Cont.
Can I hold Saint George?

                                    SIMON
Do what the hell you like.

        (She lifts Saint George out.)

                                    AZRA
How sad that you're not doing sculpture any more.

                                    SIMON
How do you know I'm not?

                                    AZRA
All I see are steel barriers.

                                    SIMON
That's my living.

                                    AZRA
This armor's amazing. Can I see the back of it to see how it's made? Will you take it off?

        (Long pause.)

                                    SIMON
Pass him over. And that small pair of snips.

        (He snips the wires holding George's breastplate)

Though why the hell I'm doing this is beyond me. There.

                                    AZRA
Fascinating. Hey...

                                    SIMON
                                  (Reacting)
I haven't seen inside this armor for...

                                    AZRA
Seven years? And the cellar where you made it, helped by Phil, belongs to someone else
now.

SIMON

You can't possibly buy this puppet theatre with Phil. He told me this show was crap. Oh yes, that was his considered opinion in 2008, when he came home for Christmas. Was Saint George meant to be George Bush? He also told me I was crap, that he'd had a miserable childhood, with me tap-tapping away in the cellar, unavailable to listen to him bleating about his teenage angst. All right?

AZRA

And what did you reply?

SIMON

I told him to piss off. I said I'd been doing the show successfully for over a year, with reasonable reviews. I said I could do without him dissing it.

AZRA

And you have, Simon. You have done without it. You've made those beautiful barriers.

    (Pause)

Did you still do the show?

SIMON

Not for long. Anita left, and my other operators were useless.

AZRA

Who's Anita?

SIMON

Don't you ever stop? Asking bloody questions?

AZRA

Are you going to tell me to piss off now?

    (Pause)

Then here's another question. Why do you think Phil said he'd had a miserable childhood?

SIMON

Probably because it was true. I was in the cellar most of the time, making armor. I need a drink.

    (Finds whisky, pours it into the mug)

One for you? Islay's finest.

    (AZRA shakes her head.)

SIMON, Cont.

Don't tell me you're a Muslim. Oh no, you're not wearing a whatsaname.

SIMON

AZRA

Do you mean a hijab? In here (her heart) I am a Muslim.

(Long pause)

SIMON

You see, back in the nineties I won a big sculpture commission. Birmingham. Heraldic beasts. I was away from home a lot. You know what happens when a man's away from home a lot.

AZRA

Depends on the man.

SIMON

Touché. But you see, Azra, I married Val thinking she was a princess.

AZRA

Like Sabra?

SIMON

Yes, I made her into a legend. Whereas in real life she was ordinary. Her tastes were ordinary. She was exceptionally beautiful and she bored me. Should have been like you, sharp and mean, keeping me on my toes.

AZRA

You're flirting with me.

SIMON

Me?

AZRA

So your marriage fell apart.

SIMON

That commission in Birmingham. Anthea, the commissioning officer, had the most amazing eyes. Do I need to explain?

AZRA

I think my hypersensitive antennae have got the drift.

SIMON

If marriage was purgatory before Anthea, it was hell afterwards. Tap tap tap. Tap tap tap. That's what dragged me out of bed the mornings I wasn't teaching. "I will make armor. I will make armor." I lost myself in these intricate patterns. The sound as the metal yielded to my design. The filing and shaping and gilding and burnishing. As each naked figure became sheathed in his panoply of gold and crowned with colorful plumes I added him to the row that accumulated like the years. Val had affairs, then left. Later I heard she'd died.

                                    AZRA

Yes.

                                    SIMON

That 'yes' again. You know all this from Phil. Are you his girlfriend?

                                    AZRA

That's not how I'd describe myself.

                                    SIMON

Oh. What a pity. For him, I mean.

                                    AZRA

Why? Do you care? Stop drinking. You've had enough.

                                    SIMON

It's all right, I'm a Christian.

                                    AZRA

So this Anita, she left you as well?

                                    SIMON

I was bloody hurt.

                                    AZRA

By Anita?

                                    SIMON

By what Phil said.

                                    AZRA

I'll ask again: do you know why he said it?

    (Pause)

Do you know what's been happening with him the last six years?

                                    SIMON

You told me. The housing department.

                                    AZRA

And before that? Before he finally found his way out of the desert?

                                    SIMON

Been travelling, has he?

                                    AZRA

You could set light to your breath.

(AZRA grabs the bottle and starts to empty it. SIMON manages to get it back.)

SIMON

Bloody hell, Azra, twenty-five quid's worth.

AZRA

And what's your son worth?

(They sit down again.)

AZRA, Cont.

Is he worth nothing? Just because he was rude to you, and negative? It's what people do in depression. I don't mean 'a bit down', I mean clinically depressed. There are no happy memories, no colours, no…reality. It's like being down in a crater—all you see is the rim.

SIMON

When was all this?

AZRA

Just after he graduated. 2007. Your last conversation was Christmas '08. I met him in 2010. He'd been in and out of 'bins' as he calls them. Just about clinging on.

SIMON

I didn't know.

AZRA

Well, he couldn't tell you. He was too ashamed.

SIMON

Why ashamed? It's an illness. Would he be ashamed if it was cancer?

AZRA

You told him to piss off, remember. He and I became friends. Lots in common. We'd both lost parents. He'd lost both. Sorry.

SIMON

How is he?

AZRA

He's okay. I think I helped. No, I did help. Five years ago, I went travelling—Morocco, Sudan, Egypt, looking for my Islamic roots. Fascinating, but I realised how British I feel and how I needed to sort Phil out.

SIMON

And you did.

AZRA

I helped him to see he could sort himself out.

                              SIMON

Thank you.

        (Breaks down)

Thank you.

        (He twists the breastplate in his hands unthinkingly. She takes it from him, gently.)

                              AZRA

You'll spoil it.

                              SIMON

I haven't seen the back of it for years. What did he mean, I never listened to him? He and I
made this. We made lots together. He was always down there helping. What did he mean?
In late afternoon the sun through the cellar window came in on the workbench. People
walking past outside made a blip, and he and I would laugh. Kate thought we were daft.
'Men,' she said, age seven.

                              AZRA

He says you had some good times together. Some.

                              SIMON

And you're his friend.

                              AZRA

Very much so. Do you disapprove? After all, I'm a Saracen. One of those dark scowling
knights in baggy trousers.

                              SIMON
                             (Laughs)

Does he know you've come here?

                              AZRA

Yes.

                              SIMON

What did he say?

                              AZRA

Not much. I think he's scared.

                              SIMON

Of me?

                              AZRA

Of how you'd be.

                                    SIMON

And you found me.

                                    AZRA

Online. Then saw, on eBay, you were selling the puppets.

                                    SIMON

I hadn't looked at them for years. I was rooting around for some bolts I needed.

        (Pause)

                                    AZRA

Simon. There's something I've held back.

                                    SIMON

For the worse?

                                    AZRA

I hope not. I don't know.

                                    SIMON

Oh. Have I got to change my opinion of you? Oh God, you're an Islamic extremist.

                                    AZRA

That's what comes to mind is it? That tells me so much about the newspapers you read—

                                    SIMON

I don't read newspapers—

                                    AZRA

—and your cultural assumptions. You think when I was a teenager, isolated in Milford,
wondering who I was, I'd turn to hate. I thought the Christian fundamentalist message of
your show was just...oh, a vestige of those medieval legends. I thought you were Don
Quixote. But maybe you really are anti-Muslim.

                                    SIMON

Azra—

                                    AZRA

Anyway, Simon, I'm not a practising Muslim. Because if I was I wouldn't...

                                    SIMON

What? Wouldn't what?

                                    AZRA

I wouldn't have married your son.

                                SIMON
What? Married? How do you mean?

                                AZRA
How do I mean? Married is married. Phil and I are married.

                                SIMON
You.

                                AZRA
Yes.

                                SIMON
And Phil.

                                AZRA
Yes. Yes. I kept my own name. I'm still Azra Dim— Simon? I thought only mothers-in-law
were affected by weddings.

                                SIMON
I have a daughter-in-law who has come to find me.

                                AZRA
In your fiery den.

                                SIMON
May I...hug you?

        (They hug.)

                                AZRA
There. Mm. You're my family.

                                SIMON
If you didn't disapprove of scotch, we could drink a toast.

                                AZRA
Sparkling water.

        (She pours some of hers into his mug.)

                                SIMON
Cheers.

                                AZRA
Cheers.

                                SIMON
To the happy couple. Long life and happiness.

                                        AZRA
Thank you.

                                       SIMON
I want to show you something.

         (He operates the window blind. Warm light floods the room.)

                                        AZRA
Awesome. What a view. And you keep it covered? I can see the London Eye. The river. St.
Paul's. Oh look. Look Simon. That's where we work. See it? That grey tower to the left of
that church spire?

                                       SIMON
I think I see it. And where do you live?

                                        AZRA
That is difficult. Oh wait. See that little group of trees to the north? Then a big chimney.
Then a big dark red thing? Just near there.

         (Pause)

Simon? Are you all right? Anyway, you'll see it. Where we live.

                                       SIMON
I don't think so.

                                        AZRA
What do you mean?

                                       SIMON
I can't do it, Azra. I can't meet him again.

                                        AZRA
He's as scared as you are.

                                       SIMON
I'm not scared. I'm just not a father anymore.

                                        AZRA
Just be yourself.

                                       SIMON
                                      (Laughs)
That's always been a recipe for mayhem.

                                        AZRA
You can't let our meeting fizzle. Simon?

(SIMON closes the curtain. The light dims.)

SIMON

I don't intend to.

AZRA

What do you mean?

SIMON

You claimed you and Phil were interested in buying my show. But you'd throw away my
script. So what would you do instead? Two inexperienced operators, one of whom hasn't a
clue and doesn't even know her own tradition?

(Pause)

AZRA

All right. I do a show called 'Régime Change 1649'. The Ottoman Empire is at its height.
Sultan Muhammad the Fourth hears of an evil, fanatical dictator who's murdered
thousands of innocent people. In Ireland. He's closed all the theatres. So Muhammad—a
great Karagoz fan, by the way—mobilizes his janissaries to invade England and hang
Cromwell. Good idea? All we need is to fit your knights with baggy trousers.

SIMON

You're a lunatic.

AZRA

You could make new armor for the English. Civil War style. Tap tap. Tap tap.

SIMON

How the hell would you operate a show like that? You and Phil and someone else?

AZRA

I was joking.

SIMON

Who is this someone else? Have they any experience?

AZRA

None whatever.

SIMON

And they haven't even joined yet. When are they expected?

AZRA

In just over four months time.

SIMON

Where from?

(Long pause)

                                    SIMON, Cont'd
Oh. Oh my God, Azra. You're with child.

                                    AZRA
                                    (Laughs)
What a quaint expression. I'm pregnant, yes. It does happen.

                                    SIMON
My grandchild.

                                    AZRA
Yes.

                                    SIMON
May I touch?

        (He does so, reverently.)

Oh wonderful.

                                    AZRA
Yes. A pity you'll never meet.

                                    SIMON
What do you mean?

                                    AZRA
A pity you'll never visit our home and get to know your granddaughter, grandson,
whichever.

                                    SIMON
The other side of the river.

                                    AZRA
You can get across. Plenty of dark slimy tunnels to crawl through.
        (Long pause)

I have to go.

                                    SIMON
Not yet. I'll get a takeaway.

                                    AZRA
To eat here? If you come home with me Phil and I will cook. Simon. Do you think I wasn't
scared, coming here?

        (She opens the curtains again.)

                              AZRA, Cont'd
Oh look.

                              SIMON
What?

                              AZRA
Bridges. Lots of bridges across the Thames. You don't have to crawl. You can walk across in
the sunshine.

                              SIMON
I'll go and change. You're growing on me.

                              AZRA
Like a wart?

                              SIMON
Exactly.

                              AZRA
These figures are growing on me. They're a family. If we remove George's armor, he's a nice
ordinary Christian, not an extremist.

                              SIMON
Won't be long.

        (Goes out)

                              AZRA
I have a family.

                    (Blackout)

Ocean Memories

Andrew Graber

Loving a Shadow

Marge Piercy

There are people who spin
romance around the one they
didn't bed, move in with or wed.

The one they didn't choose
or who had little interest in them
shines brighter in memory

than any lover in the flesh.
Petrarch created the model.
I knew a woman who wrote

endless poems about a boy
she'd known who had died
young so never grew past

her, someone she never
even kissed. Perfect object
for adoration without price:

never gained a pound or lost
a job, never had kids or went
to jail. What man could compare?

Throw It Out, They Say

Marge Piercy

Many of us have trouble with
discarding some of our objects—
magazines. clothes perhaps.

I can't bear to throw out books.
Maybe I'll reread *Moby Dick*
or *Ulysses* one more time.

Shakespeare can't go. What about
a recent novel reviews touted
that stalled me in chapter three.

I write books and shudder to imagine
people tossing them in the trash.
I revere books. They're piggy banks

of lives, vaults of the human past.
How can I cheerfully discard some
one's heart and mind, preserved?

E'er the Night

Karen Colstrom

THE WALLACE HOUSE OF PAIN

S.M. Stevens

SYNOPSIS

A young man brings a series of interesting friends to dinner at his father's house as he works up the courage to come out to him.

CHARACTERS

XANDER (ALEXANDER), a 28-year-old White activist
TERRANCE, Xander's friend, Black with bleached blonde hair
JIM WALLACE, Xander's father
KATHY WALLACE, Xander's stepmother
SUNNY, mixed-race friend and sometimes lover of Xander
JESSICA, Colombian-American friend of Xander
CHARLEY, White friend and eventual girlfriend of Xander
BUWAN, friend of Xander, bronze-skinned

SETTING

A modest borough in a typical U.S. city

TIME

The present

SCENE 1

JIM's house; the exterior of the front door and landing, and the interior of the dining room, are visible. A swinging door in the dining room leads to the kitchen. XANDER and TERRANCE approach the front door; Terrance holds a six-pack of beer.

XANDER

Remember what I relayed when I extended this invitation -- we don't choose our parents. My Dad isn't the most liberal guy in the world.

TERRANCE

Xander, I'm sure I've handled worse in thirty years. But if he's so bad, why are you dragging me with you?

XANDER

(Drumming his fingers on his thigh)

Truth be told, having someone else there prevents the conversation from devolving into a farce of familial relations. (Shrugs) In other words, it sucks and I need moral support.

(KATHY opens the door and stands in the doorway.)

KATHY

Hello, hello! How are you?

(She clutches XANDER's forearm.)

XANDER

Reasonable.

KATHY

(In a low voice)

I'm so glad you came. These monthly dinners mean a lot to Jim.

(At a normal volume)

I know you had to work late, so I've got supper all ready. Hungry?

(KATHY pulls XANDER inside and repeats the maneuver with TERRANCE, who hands her the six-pack.)

And you're Terrance, of course. I'm Kathy. I love your hair. I love the contrast with your skin color.

TERRANCE

I'm glad you like it. Unlike my skin color, I did pick out the hair color.

KATHY

You're funny! I'm a hair stylist, you know. Maybe I can do your hair sometime.

(Leads them into the dining room)

TERRANCE

No offense, Mrs. Wallace, but my mother always told me, never let a white person touch my hair.

(XANDER starts to laugh but stops as JIM enters)

XANDER

Dad.

JIM

Alex.

TERRANCE

Terrance Washington, sir. Pleased to meet you.

(JIM assesses TERRANCE head to toe. Releases a barely audible grunt and shakes hands.)

JIM
Come on, let's eat. Kathy, can you get the food going sometime this century?

KATHY
It's all ready, Jim, I'll get it now.

(The men sit at the dining room table. KATHY ferries dishes between the kitchen and dining room.)

TERRANCE
(Looks at XANDER and raises an eyebrow)

Alex?

JIM
That's his name. It's a perfectly good one, picked out by his mother, and I see no reason to change it.

XANDER
You see, Terrance, even at twenty-eight, I'm apparently not mature enough to select the moniker I prefer. So here I remain Alex whilst everywhere else, I am Xander.

(KATHY enters from kitchen with three beer bottles)

KATHY
Look, Jim, Terrance brought us some beer. Who's having one?

(XANDER takes two and passes one to TERRANCE.)

JIM
I'll have my usual.

(KATHY returns to the kitchen and brings back a Bud Lite.)

XANDER
My father thinks drinking imported beer converts previously respectable God-fearing citizens into socialists and iconoclasts. Never mind that Anheuser-Busch is owned by a Belgian-Brazilian company now.

JIM
But it's still brewed here.

TERRANCE
No worries, it's all good.

(After a silence interrupted only by serving spoons clinking against bowls and plates, KATHY clears her throat.)

KATHY
Terrance, so you work with Alex at the Wildlife Preservation—what is it again?

TERRANCE
The Wilderness Protection Society. I moved here to take the job six months ago.

JIM
So you're a tree-hugger, too.

TERRANCE
Well, sir, I do believe the human race is destroying the planet, and, if we don't change our ways soon, the Earth won't sustain future generations.

JIM
I think this global warming stuff is a bunch of BS. How can it be getting warmer if it's snowing more than ever, and some winters are colder than a witch's tit.

TERRANCE
It's simple science, actually. Warmer temperatures mean more moisture in the air which means—

XANDER
Terrance, conserve your breath.

JIM
Anyway, I thought your job (to XANDER) was to save the birds and the bees or some such shit.

KATHY
Jim, language! Alex has explained this before. To save the animals, you have to save the planet, too. Terrance, why don't you tell us what you do at work?

TERRANCE
Sure. Like everyone at Wilderness Protection, my job revolves around monitoring what's going on with the climate and the environment, and motivating people to make positive changes to lessen our impact on the natural world. My focus is communications. Xander's actually got the more important job, because he's on the front lines organizing the masses and holding the bad guys accountable for their misdeeds.

JIM
And by 'misdeeds' you mean somebody trying to make an honest living.

XANDER
No, Dad, he means people like the city's biggest developer, who gleefully circumvents environmental regulations whenever he pleases to convert another piece of pristine wilderness into condos or a factory. We're fighting him right now on —

JIM

And what's wrong with factories? They give a lot of hard-working people decent jobs.

XANDER

My dad's a supervisor at the paper mill.

TERRANCE

Nothing's wrong with factories per se — we need them. But there are plenty of brownfield sites that could be used to site new factories and other big projects instead of ruining undeveloped wilderness.

JIM

Brownfield? What the hell is a brownfield? Sounds shitty to me.

  (Laughs into XANDER's face. XANDER shuts his eyes. They continue eating, in
  silence until KATHY stands and gathers a few dishes.)

KATHY

I'm going to warm up the dessert.

TERRANCE

Let me help.

JIM

Go on and help, son.

  (KATHY and TERRANCE exit into kitchen.)

Alex, how long are you going to keep this up?

XANDER

What, Dad? What is it this time?

  (He tries to stare his father down but breaks his gaze)

JIM

The job. When are you going to get a real job at a real company? Stop thinking about yourself and plan for your future. That means you might have to have a job you care (sarcastic emphasis) less about but that puts you in a better position to provide for a family.

XANDER

I've told you myriad times. For a nonprofit, Wilderness Protection compensates well and offers substantial benefits. It is a legitimate job, and the person I marry will understand that and support my career choice.

                                    JIM

No, you don't get it. It's not all about you. The world doesn't revolve around you.
Sometimes you have to do things you don't want to do.

        (XANDER shakes salt onto the table and plays with the crystals)

All you millennials are the same. Everyone's special. Everyone gets a trophy just for
showing up. Everyone's entitled to whatever they want. Well, guess what? Life isn't like
that, and the sooner you realize it, the better off you'll be.

Your generation had it so easy because your mother did everything for you. When I was a
kid, I mowed lawns and delivered newspapers to make a buck and get the things I wanted.
We didn't sit around on our asses all day on Facebook and whatever else it is you use. By
the time I was your age, I had a wife and three kids to feed. That makes you grow up real
fast. You could—

        (KATHY and TERRANCE return and sit. JIM faces TERRANCE, draping his arm
        across his chair as if preparing to ask about Sunday's football game. XANDER
        squirms.)

                                    JIM

What's up with the hair, son? And the earrings?

                                  XANDER

His name is Terrance, Dad.

                                    JIM

He knows who I'm talking to. Don't you?

        (TERRANCE nods, eyes narrowing.)

You trying to make a statement? Is that what all the, you know, certain types of guys wear
these days?

                                  XANDER

Are you asking if he's gay? Don't you think that's a rather personal question to ask a guest?

                                    JIM

I'm just curious. I don't have anything against the fa—against the homosexuals, isn't that
right, Kathy?

                                   KATHY

We think one of the guys on Jim's crew is gay. And he's got Mexicans, African-Americans
and, what is it, Jim?—oh right, Brazilians working for him, too.

                                    JIM

That's right. And no one makes a big deal of it. As long as he gets his job done, and as long
as he's not illegal, I don't care what color he is or who he—who he spends time with.

XANDER
And with that ringing endorsement, the world's gay and minority populations sighed in
relief.

(Gestures with his arms like a speaker on a stage)

KATHY
Alex, why are you so angry? You're the one who brought it up.

XANDER
I'm not angry. I'm exceptionally disinterested because the conversation here never
changes. But thank you for dinner, Kathy. It was delectable. A pleasure as always.

KATHY
But we have brownies and ice cream. The brownies should be warm now.

TERRANCE
Smells great, but I'm watching my figure.

XANDER
Okay. Until next time then.

(XANDER and TERRANCE exit)

(Blackout)

SCENE 2
        Immediately after. XANDER and TERRANCE are in Terrance's car. TERRANCE
        drives.

XANDER

At least he didn't admonish me to get a haircut.

TERRANCE
'Not the most liberal guy'? You could have been more specific, like—for starters—warning
me he was a climate change denier.

XANDER
(pulls his lips back in fake consternation)

But then I would have had to warn you he's also a racist, a sexist, a xenophobe, and a
homophobe, and the ride wasn't nearly long enough for all that.

TERRANCE
I'm glad you think this is funny. You basically threw me to the wolves, pitched me in the
lion's den, dangled me out there like bait.

                              XANDER
                              (Joking)

Appalling use of clichés.

        (Seriously)

But I am truly sorry for putting you in that position. I let my trepidation skew my moral
code, and I apologize.

                              TERRANCE
It's all right.

                              XANDER
        (Chuckles and counts on his fingers)

I don't know which alarmed him more—the hair, the earrings, the tree-hugging job, or your
race.

                              TERRANCE
You suck, you know that? But I have to ask: Why do you keep going back every month?

                              XANDER
I guess because I'm the only one he's got. One of my sisters moved three states away and
the other one stopped coming several months back. She says it's too arduous to pack up
her husband and two kids for a quick meal.

        (Car stops. XANDER closes his eyes and drawls as if in a trance.)

Intolerance reigns, in the Wallace house of pain. Will peace ever come?

                              TERRANCE
What do you call those little ditties again?

                              XANDER
A haiku, dude. It's not a ditty. A ditty is a song.

                              TERRANCE
Remind me why you find satisfaction in making up one of the world's shortest poems.

                              XANDER
I don't seek them out. They pop into my head when I least expect it. I've had this affliction
since fifth grade when I penned my first haiku. Maybe it stuck with me because somewhere
in the forbidden area of my psyche, I'm still crushing on my fifth-grade teacher.

                              TERRANCE
What was her name?

                              XANDER
His name.

TERRANCE

You're gay? But I've seen you with women.

XANDER

Technically, I'm bi. But don't worry, I'm not into you. (Smirks)

TERRANCE

Not worried. And I'm guessing your dad doesn't know?

XANDER

Correct assumption.

TERRANCE

Your sisters?

XANDER

Telling them would be tantamount to telling my dad.

TERRANCE

Now that I've met your old man, I can see why you're keeping it quiet.

XANDER

I will tell him someday. I have to. It's damaging to one's soul to live a lie. And it's not like his view of me could get any lower. But I have to work up to it.

TERRANCE

Hmm.

(XANDER shows no sign of leaving, so TERRANCE flicks his hand toward the passenger door.)

Can you get out, so I can go home and have a break before I have to see your sorry ass at work in a few hours?

(XANDER smiles and opens the car door)

(Blackout)

SCENE 3

The backyard of JIM's home. JIM and KATHY sit at a patio table. XANDER and SUNNY enter the back yard, SUNNY holding a gift bag. KATHY awkwardly hugs XANDER.

KATHY

Alex, how are you?

                              XANDER
Phlegmatic, I hope. You?

        (KATHY holds out her arms to SUNNY. They hug.)

                              KATHY
Sunny, so nice to meet you!

                              SUNNY
I brought this for you.

                              KATHY
        (Pulls a candle from the bag and sniffs, closing her eyes in approval)

You shouldn't have.

                              SUNNY
It's a soy candle so it burns cleaner and doesn't have any petroleum-based ingredients. The
vanilla and sandalwood scents create an atmosphere of relaxation and serenity.

                              KATHY
I love it.

        (XANDER and JIM shrug at each other. SUNNY approaches JIM and forces an
        awkward hug)

                              JIM
Well, sit down, sit down. We thought we'd enjoy the beautiful day before we start cooking.

                              XANDER
You're in an unexpectedly jolly mood today.

                              JIM
I got a big fat bonus at work yesterday; the sun is shining, and my only son is here to visit.
What's not to be happy about?

        (JIM opens a cooler and motions for them to dig in. XANDER lifts a light beer to
        SUNNY as proof of his willingness to be sociable. He hands SUNNY a wine spritzer
        and downs half his beer in two gulps.)

                              KATHY
So, are you two dating?

        (SUNNY and XANDER laugh. XANDER grabs SUNNY's hand with a look that says
        'Just go with it.')

                              XANDER
Sunny is the most amazing person I know, and we have a very special relationship.

(KATHY nods as if that explains everything.)

                              KATHY
Tell me, where did you have your first date? I love first date stories.

         (SUNNY and XANDER laugh again. KATHY's smile fades. SUNNY touches
         KATHY's arm.)

                              SUNNY
We're only laughing because people don't really date anymore. We all hang out in groups
and sometimes, if it's meant to be, we connect in a meaningful way.

                              KATHY
Hmm.

         (KATHY glances around, reaches out and touches the top of Sunny's head, pressing
         down on their short Afro.)

I just love Black hair. It's so springy. I never get to work with it at the salon.

         (XANDER clears his throat. KATHY yanks her hand back.)

And I love your necklace!

                              XANDER
By the way, I should inform you that Sunny is non-binary and prefers to go by 'they'
instead of 'she'.

         (Pops open a second beer)

                              JIM
She what?

                              KATHY
She wants to be called 'they' like there's two of her?

         (SUNNY shakes their head at XANDER, inhales deeply and smiles with effort at
         KATHY.)

                              SUNNY
Don't worry, Mrs. Wallace, I don't have multiple personalities or anything. What Xander
means is, I don't identify with either the female or male gender.

                              KATHY
So, you're not a woman? You dress like one.

                              SUNNY
I wear what feels right to me, which is generally what people consider women's clothing.
But I prefer to think of myself as neither sex. I'm just me. I just am.

                                JIM

Do you have female body parts or don't you?

        (KATHY slaps JIM's arm. JIM shrugs.)

It's a simple question. If you're born with girl parts, you're female. If you're born with boy parts, you're male. I paid attention that day in high school biology.

                              XANDER

You don't have to ans—

                               SUNNY

It's okay, Xan. The parts I was born with are my business, Mr. Wallace. What matters is that today, I prefer not to be thought of as male or female.

                               KATHY

But if you're not male or female, not to be rude but…do you like men or women?

                               SUNNY

That's a completely different thing, but to answer your question, I like both.

                                JIM

Could have seen that one coming.

                              XANDER

Sunny is attracted to all genders, including cisgender men and women, transgender men and women, and agender and gender nonconforming individuals. It's called being pansexual.

                               KATHY

Pansexual? I've never heard of that. What does it mean?

                                JIM

It means she'll do it with anybody or anything including probably pots and pans.

                               SUNNY

Funny. I've never heard that one before. (Turns to KATHY) Would you like me to explain how people today define how they love?

                               KATHY

Sure. (Drawing out the word)

                               SUNNY

We still have regular heterosexuals—men who love women and women who love men.

                                JIM

Thank God for small favors.

                                    SUNNY
Then we have homosexuals which includes gays and lesbians—men who like men, women
who like women. We've got bisexuals—people who like both men and women and
sometimes other genders.

                                    KATHY
What other genders are there? You mean like transsexuals, is that what they're called?

          (KATHY bounces in her seat like a student who wants the teacher to pick her.
          XANDER smiles.)

                                    SUNNY
Today, they're called transgender people or simply trans.

                                    KATHY
You're obviously a lovely person, Sunny, but I have to admit, sometimes it feels like young
people are looking for attention with all of these crazy labels. It's like people want their
own special, new identity to make them stand out.

                                    XANDER
Is that so deplorable? Wanting to be unique?

                                    KATHY
I guess not. But in our day, we had regular men, regular women and David Bowie. That was
it. And that was plenty.

                                    SUNNY
This doesn't need to be complicated, Mrs. Wallace. People come in many shapes and sizes.
As you're happily married, it shouldn't matter to you what someone else's sexual
orientation is anyway.

                                    JIM
I'm gonna get the burgers. (Exits)

                                    KATHY
Can I ask a question? Hopefully it's not too personal. How can you be attracted to more
than one gender? Doesn't one feel right and one feel wrong?

                                    SUNNY
Kathy. Does a pickle taste the same to you as a doughnut?

          (XANDER suppresses a laugh)

                                    KATHY
Of course not.

                                    SUNNY
Do you like them both?

KATHY

I prefer doughnuts, to be honest. I have a sweet tooth.

SUNNY

Perfect. Some people like the taste of pickles, some prefer doughnuts. I happen to like both. I might even like a pickle-flavored doughnut if one existed. It doesn't make me weird. It means I have broader tastes than some people.

KATHY

> (Her face twists in puzzlement. She stands and brushes imaginary specks off her shorts.)

Well, I'm going to bring out the food, and we'll get this cookout going.

> (KATHY exits into the house. XANDER stands and kisses SUNNY on the head.)

XANDER

You're incomparable, Sunny Winston. But you know that.

SUNNY

We should help bring the food out.

XANDER

No, don't. They probably need a minute to decompress. We'll do the cleaning up after we eat.

> (XANDER sits, stretches his legs and wiggles his feet. SUNNY curls their legs up underneath them and closes their eyes. JIM and KATHY return with platters of food. They eat.)

JIM

Sunny, what do you do for work?

> (His eyes plead for this subject to be innocuous)

SUNNY

I sell solar energy systems.

JIM

You've got the name for it.

SUNNY

I know, right?

XANDER

And the disposition.

KATHY

Someone down the street has solar panels on their house. They don’t look that bad.

SUNNY

I think they’re beautiful. They blend right into dark roofs, plus they prevent air pollution and make the planet healthier. What’s not to love?

JIM

They’re too expensive. I got a quote once because a guy at work’s son is in solar.

(XANDER stares wide-eyed at his father)

It was going to take almost eight years for the panels to be paid off.

SUNNY

Jim, have you made any purchases lately that actually pay for themselves?

(JIM shakes his head slowly as if being lured into a trap)

Everyone knows a new car loses twenty percent of its value in the first year.

(JIM nods once)

That’s money spent that you’ll never get back. So isn’t getting paid back over eight years better than not being paid back at all?

JIM

When you put it that way—

SUNNY

Right? When you’re ready for a new quote, you let me know. I’ll fix you up with the best deal out there.

JIM

(to XANDER, with admiration)

Got a smart one here, don’t you.

KATHY

Sunny, come inside and let me show you the house. There are some pictures of Alex and his Dad I bet you’ll love.

(KATHY and SUNNY collect some of the dishes and exit)

XANDER

Dad, not to make you uncomfortable, but what do you think about Sunny’s attraction to men and women? Do you think it abnormally bizarre, or can you understand a tad how someone might love someone else of the same sex?

                                    JIM

What do I think? I'd rather not think about it at all. She seems great, but come on, Alex. If
you guys are dating, how do you feel knowing she's been with other women and
transsexuals and who knows what? That's worse than being gay and gay is weird enough.
Men loving men just isn't natural.

                                  XANDER

But it is, actually. Homosexual relations are, in fact, antediluvian. Cave paintings depict
homosexual relationships thousands of years Before Christ. Archaeologists have uncovered
similar images all over Europe and Africa, from the earliest civilizations. It's well-known
men in ancient Greece had lifelong relationships with each other. And this was all B.C.

                                    JIM

Maybe the coming of Christ shamed them straight.

                                  XANDER

No, actually the trend continued A.C. Emperor Nero of Rome married two men,
Pythagoras and Sporus. How about that?

                                    JIM

Polygamy? Tsk. That's bad.

                                  XANDER

The buried city of Pompeii revealed artwork showing men copulating with men and women
with women. And we haven't even left the first century yet.

                                    JIM

Okay, you can stop the history lesson. I get it. It's been around a long time.

But that doesn't mean they need to broadcast it, marching around in skimpy outfits,
demanding to be treated equally at the same time they want everyone to notice how
different they are. I don't wanna know who people vote for. I don't wanna know how much
money they make. And I don't wanna know who they're sleeping with. Why can't we all just
live our lives and not bother each other?

                                  XANDER

Because, Dad, gay people are still discriminated against in our contumelious society.
They're still denied some of the rights straight people take for granted.

                                    JIM

They got gay marriage, didn't they? What else do they need? Sometimes it seems like
people just like the fight. (Stands) Well, thanks for stopping by. That Sunny's an interesting
one. Not shy, is she?

                                  XANDER

How do you feel about me and Sunny dating, them being Black and all?

JIM

Jesus, you can't stop, can you? It's like you keep picking at a scab, making it worse. I don't care about her skin color. There. Happy? (Stomps into the house)

(Blackout)

SCENE 4

>The dining room. JIM and KATHY sit on one side of the table, XANDER and JESS on the other. They are mid-meal. XANDER is visibly preoccupied. JESS purposely drops her napkin on the floor, then leans in toward Xander and speaks softly as she picks it up.

JESS

You sure you're ready for this?

>(Xander shrugs)

I'll take that as a yes. You've got this.

>(She straightens up and looks up JIM and KATHY)

KATHY

Jess, you've got a beautiful tan. Do you go to a tanning salon?

JESS

No, this is my normal color.

JIM

You Mexican? Puerto Rican?

JESS

I'm American, born and raised here. But my parents are from Colombia, hence the year-round tan.

KATHY

Colombia? Like the coffee growers I see on the TV ads?

JESS

Well, yes... . That's the same country, and Colombia is known for its coffee. But my family aren't farmers. My father is a lawyer, and my mother runs a dental office.

XANDER

Do you by chance watch Modern Family? The actor Sofia Vergara is Colombian. So they export more than coffee.

>(JESS laughs but no one else does.)

KATHY

I know her! She's on the cover of the magazines in the salon all the time! She's so beautiful. But why don't you sound like her?

XANDER

Born and bred here, Kathy, did you not hear her say that? Jess is American and was born here.

(XANDER shrinks back into his thoughts)

JIM

So you said you're an accountant at a big-deal real estate firm in the financial district. You're pretty ambitious for your generation. It's good to see a young person who cares about the company they work for. Most people your age just float along, hopping between jobs, no loyalty, trying to find themselves. Lazy is what they are, because they got those ridiculous trophies as kids, just for showing up. No one should get a trophy for that.

KATHY

It does make the kids expect good things like an award or a treat without having to earn it.

JIM

Entitlement, Kathy, that's what it's called.

JESS

You know, sometimes millennials change jobs a lot because we want to be passionate about what we do. Accounting may sound dull, but I love my job. If I didn't, I'd move on because life is too short to toil away at something you don't love. It's that old cliché. We want to work to live, not live to work.

KATHY

I've never heard that before. I like it. And I love my job, too.

JIM

But my guys at the factory, the younger ones, are so demanding. They all want flexible hours and better benefits.

JESS

Doesn't everyone? Maybe the difference is that our generation is willing to ask for it.

JIM

One of our office ladies actually asked management to let her work from home. (Laughs) Can you imagine that? We're a damn factory. Can't really run a production line if half the people work somewhere else.

(Sits back, grinning, as if he has single-handedly debunked the entire concept of telecommuting.)

And so many of you people take the feel-good job instead of the one that's best for their family.

(JIM stares at XANDER. JESS slowly places her fork down.)

                              JESS
Millennials were brought up to give back, to do good. We're more socially engaged. So a job choice that seems selfish to one person might seem noble and generous to someone else.

                              KATHY
(Cautiously, as if asking about a social disease)

How are you socially engaged?

        (JIM glares at KATHY.)

                              JESS
Well, a bunch of us went to a rally a few weeks ago to protest racial profiling in the city's police department, and—

                              JIM
So let me guess. You sympathize with the Blacks who complain about being stopped more by the police, even though they commit more crimes? And while we're at it, why don't we coddle the illegal aliens flooding across the border?

                              JESS
Oh no, I'm against illegal immigration. You wouldn't believe how much it costs us taxpayers.

                              JIM
Exactly. It's a scourge on our society. I wish they would all stay home. You don't see us rushing their borders.

                              KATHY
I heard there's a Women's March this weekend.

                              JESS
Yeah, a bunch of us are actually going.

                              JIM
People who protest should stay home and worry about their own families instead of sticking their noses in other people's business.

                              KATHY
I'm thinking I might go. Sally and Linda are going, and they invited me.

        (JIM's face contorts.)

Just to see what the fuss is about.

        (Awkward silence. JESS looks at XANDER.)

                              JESS
So Xander, isn't there something important you want to tell your father?

        (XANDER looks ill. He stares at his plate.)

                            XANDER
Dad, I—I—well—

                              JIM
Spit it out, son.

                            XANDER
I'm dating Jess.

                            KATHY
That's wonderful, isn't it, Jim? But what about—(whispers) Sunny?

                            XANDER
Oh. Sunny and I were never really dating.

        (JESS raises her eyebrows and places a hand on his arm.)

                             JESS
Aw, that's sweet of you to say, but let's be honest, Xan. (faces JIM) We're just really, really, old, good friends. Xander hasn't found his one true love yet. That's what he wanted to tell you about. Who he's hoping to find.

        (She nudges his foot under the table. He is frozen. JESS appears to come to a
        conclusion in her head. She reaches for his hand under the table and squeezes.)

Kathy. Jim. Thank you so much for dinner. The food was great. Would it be rude if we made an early exit? I have to be at work at seven in the morning.

        (XANDER flies from the house like a thoroughbred released from the starting gate)

                          (Blackout)

SCENE 5
        Jim's dining room. JIM and KATHY sit on one side of the table, XANDER and
        CHARLEY on the other. They are mid-meal.

                            KATHY
Alex, guess what I did? (Glances nervously at JIM, then back to XANDER) I went to a protest—that Women's March—with my girlfriends.

                           CHARLEY
That's so cool, Kathy. Did you like it?

KATHY

I did! I never thought much about fighting for a cause. I think a lot of us accept whatever life dishes out. But it made me feel so...strong? Happy? (Shakes her head and laughs)

CHARLEY

Empowered. Is that what you felt?

KATHY

Yes. That's it exactly, Charley. Empowered.

CHARLEY

I know what you mean. I only went to my first protest a while ago, after meeting Xander.

(Beams at XANDER but his face is blank)

It's such a simple concept—join a group to say something's wrong—but so many of us never even think about doing it. I see the world in a whole new way now.

(CHARLEY trails off. JIM stares at the fork making trips back and forth from his plate to his mouth. XANDER's eyes alternate between his dad and the far wall.)

CHARLEY

(Nudges Xander's arm)

Xan. Isn't that great that Kathy went to her first protest?

XANDER

Sure, one has to start somewhere. But to make a material difference, you must do more than merely show up.

KATHY

What do you mean?

XANDER

(Closes his eyes and intones a haiku)

Donate to the cause. Write letters to media. Call legislators.

(He opens his eyes and smiles at CHARLEY before turning to KATHY.)

Most of all, keep showing up. To march, to volunteer, to be seen and heard.

CHARLEY

Our last protest was the candlelight vigil for Jamal Taylor, the teenager shot by the police.

(JIM stares accusingly at CHARLEY. Her hand flies to her nose ring, then to a mole under her lip, which she rubs with her thumb.)

                                  JIM
That the Black kid who went after the officer with a switchblade?

                                XANDER
Dad, he didn't brandish a knife. He didn't even have one. It was a racially motivated,
aggravated assault by the police, no debate about it. And the Mayor is a travesty on two
legs. For all his effluence, he's done nothing about Jamal Taylor just like he's done nothing
about rampant profiling in the police department.

                                 KATHY
But if he had a knife, it wouldn't have mattered what color skin he had, would it? I don't
see Black or White. I tell myself we're all the same.

                                XANDER
He didn't ha—

        (Stops and flashes CHARLEY a wry smile, his expression suggesting they two alone
        grasp reality)

                                 KATHY
Charley, can I ask you a personal question? Did you grow up with African-Americans and
other races, or was your town all white?

                               CHARLEY
Well, as a kid I lived in a mostly white suburb, but in high school, I lived here in the city
with kids of all races.

                                 KATHY
And would you say you see color because of that, or that you don't see color because of
that?

        (XANDER and JIM regard KATHY with surprise. CHARLEY twirls her fork a few
        times before putting it down.)

                               CHARLEY
Both, I guess. I definitely became more aware of different races during high school. And I
felt like an outsider sometimes. But I also made some great friends on the cross-country
team including a Black girl and an Asian boy. So, in the end, it made me see color, but also
realize that it doesn't matter.

                                XANDER
To you. Color doesn't matter to you. But you don't discount the importance of race or
pretend it has no bearing on the thought processes and behaviors of many people.

        (CHARLEY nods uncertainly. KATHY hangs on XANDER's words.)

You can't simply pronounce that color doesn't matter. (Sounds weary at pointing out the
same issues again) It's not adequate to not be racist. Doing nothing means you condone the

XANDER, Cont'd
behavior. You have to be decidedly anti-racist. You have to speak up when you witness racist behavior.

KATHY
I admit I've turned my head or shut my mouth when a friend said something mean about a minority person. Next time, I'll try to say something.

XANDER
That would be commendable, Kathy. Remember, you have the power to help change the world for the better.

(KATHY looks mildly proud. JIM glances from one to the other, his look impossible to decipher. They continue eating in silence.)

(Blackout)

SCENE 6
The living room of XANDER's apartment. XANDER and CHARLEY sit on a couch, XANDER holds a TV remote.

CHARLEY
Dinner went well, don't you think? Did you get what you wanted?

XANDER

(Cocks his head as if the concept were new to him.)

I guess if my desire was a relatively peaceful meal, then yes—I got what I wanted.

CHARLEY
But...

XANDER
If I sought some kind of bond with my dad, even a tenuous one, then I didn't.

CHARLEY
Hmm. What do you want from your dad, Xan?

XANDER
I guess the ultimate would be for him to sanction my career choice and accept me for who I am, including my sexuality. But that's unlikely. He'll never move further along the spectrum of empathy and understanding.

CHARLEY
Have you ever talked to him about your mother's death?

XANDER

What's that got to do with anything?

CHARLEY

It seems like maybe you have to deal with the elephant in the room before you can move on to other things. You've got this shared demon in your past that no one's talking about.

XANDER

We've had years in which to talk about it so it's reasonably safe to assume no one wants to. He's never asked how I felt. Not once.

CHARLEY

You know, when my parents died, I never thought about how it affected my grandparents. One day, cross-country practice was canceled, so I got home early, and I heard Gram in her bedroom, bawling her eyes out. I was too afraid to talk to her, so I snuck out and wandered around the neighborhood for an hour. I think she may have known, because that night, Gramps and I had a talk. We liked to sit on our little porch, and it was a hot night, so we're out there under the moon and he starts talking about Mom.

He said 'I know you miss your mom and dad. You must know Edith and I miss them, too. Jane was our little girl, and a part of who we are, so, when we lost her, it left a gaping hole. Don't worry if you catch one of us grieving. It's all normal. But now we have you, and you're helping make us whole again.' Then he said, 'I'm not telling you this to upset you. We are each responsible for our own happiness.'

I didn't understand what he meant for a long time.

XANDER

But you do now?

CHARLEY

I think so. He was telling me their sadness was not my burden. (Clears her throat) There's a point to my story. Death changes everyone. At fifteen, I was too selfish to see their pain—

XANDER

I beg to differ. You were human and young and in pain yourself.

CHARLEY

Okay. But I feel like people spend a lot of time and energy trying to make sense of death. But we do it alone. It's weird and sad that when a family should pull together, sometimes we push each other away.

XANDER

It takes two to tango.

CHARLEY

I just don't think you should waste a parent unless it's truly a lost cause.

                              XANDER
Maybe it is.

                              CHARLEY
Then why, Xander, do you keep going back?

        (XANDER startles, then turns to the TV and picks up the remote.)

                              CHARLEY
        (Takes the remote from his hand)

Wait. I want to say something else. I don't think you're desperate for your father's
approval. I think you're desperate for his love. I feel guilty because I'm not sure I loved my
parents enough when they were here. And I feel sad because I'm not sure they loved me
enough.

                              XANDER
You have to stop concerning yourself with that. What we have has to be enough.

                              CHARLEY
I know. But what if you don't know how much you have? And you can still find out?

                         (Blackout)

SCENE 7
        JIM's dining room. JIM, KATHY, XANDER and BUWAN sit at the table. The meal
        is almost complete. The mood is light. XANDER and BUWAN are mildly drunk.
        Several beer bottles litter the table. BUWAN leans back, pats his belly and belches.

                              XANDER
Good one.

        (He hiccups and laughs)

                              KATHY
So what are you boys up to after this?

                              BUWAN
                         (Excitedly)
We're headed in town for the Black Lives Matter protest.

        (JIM grunts)

                              KATHY
I saw last night's protest on the news. It was scary, how the protestors threatened the
police.

XANDER

Who's more threatening or intimidating, Kathy—an individual armed with nothing but a homemade sign, or a cop sporting a bulletproof vest, helmet and shield? Regardless, we protestors are not trying to scare the police. We're trying to wake them up. Plus, the police are already scared. That's why they and the politicians and all the powers-that-be continue to oppress minorities—out of fear that empowered minorities will take something away from them.

KATHY

Like what?

XANDER

I don't know—whatever matters most to them. Their jobs, their livelihoods, their women, their men, their neighborhoods.

BUWAN

Their control.

KATHY

Do you think tonight's protest will be dangerous?

XANDER

It depends on how the cops comport themselves. If they push the crowds or throw teargas or fire rubber bullets, people will fight back.

JIM
(Face puckering)
No son of mine better raise a hand toward a cop. I raised you better than that.

XANDER
(Hiccups)

Did you? Raise me, I mean?

JIM

What the hell is that supposed to mean?

XANDER

Let's be honest, Dad. Mom raised me. Not you. Charley insists we should talk about Mom. (Hiccups again) 'Cause we never have.

(JIM's eyes register a beat of pain. KATHY shrinks into her seat. BUWAN continues eating, not looking but clearly listening to the father-son exchange.)

JIM

This is hardly the time for that.

XANDER

Yeah, why rush it? It's only been sixteen years since she died.

JIM

You're out of line, Alex.

XANDER

Maybe you're out of line too. Why didn't you let me mourn her? She was my mother!

JIM

It's time for you to go.

(JIM ushers XANDER to the door, BUWAN trailing behind)

(Blackout)

SCENE 8

The wide, front steps of the police station. JIM stands by the door. XANDER exits the station wearing the same clothes as in the previous scene. He is dusty and disheveled, his eyes bloodshot and his hair messy. The sound of passing cars and other city noises are heard occasionally.

XANDER
(Steeling himself, walks over to JIM and holds out his hand)

Thanks for bailing me out, Dad. I'll pay you back, obviously. I guess they might drop the charges, so that's good.

(Lowers his hand when JIM doesn't shake it)

JIM

At least it's Sunday so I didn't have to leave work to rescue my wayward son.

XANDER

I can take the train home.

JIM

I'm here. I might as well drive you.

(A deep cough wracks Xander's body)

JIM

Let's get you out of here. (Thinks) Actually, let's sit.

(He goes to the side of the wide steps and sits. XANDER stiffens, but eases himself down beside JIM, every muscle complaining.)

JIM

Son, what's going on?

XANDER

The protest got a bit out of hand. The cops started arresting everyone, even if they didn't see you causing mayhem. Buwan got arrested too. Not sure where he ended up--(trails off)

JIM

Yeah, I got that. What I want to know is, why? You were such a sweet kid.

(XANDER turns and stares at JIM.)

Always helping the other kids, saving every little damn animal. Now it seems like you're angry all the time.

(XANDER drops his head.)

You're more like me than you think. Not because you got arrested—that was stupid. But you're a fighter. How do you think I survived fifteen years of living with a man who used me as a punching bag? How do you think I managed to protect my little sister? By taking my licks and getting a very thick skin. I vowed I'd survive if only to prove him wrong—that I wasn't a piece of shit like he said.

XANDER

So you were cold and hard with me to make me tougher? Really? Thank God I had Mom to balance you out.

(JIM groans softly.)

Maybe you're more like your father than you realize.

(JIM flinches.)

JIM

I hope to hell not. When I proposed to your mother, she made me promise I wouldn't repeat the cycle of abuse. She said she wasn't going to live in fear of me turning into my father. I thought I did all right. I never raised a finger to you kids.

XANDER

(Clears his irritated throat)

You spanked me the time I spilled juice on the new rug after Mom told me not to leave the kitchen.

JIM

(Laughs, making XANDER look at him with surprise)

I thought Emma was going to spank me for spanking you—she was so mad. Anyway, I can't have you turning out like your grandfather. Tell me that's not what's going on here.

                                XANDER
(Shakes his head and meets JIM's gaze.)

No, Dad. I'm not feeling violent. I have no predisposition to hurt anyone. I'm just
extremely frustrated lately.

     (Plants his elbows on his thighs and rests his head in his hands, fingers weaving
     through his hair)

                                 JIM
Okay. Tell me. Why the frustration?

                                XANDER
You do not want to have this conversation, trust me.

                                 JIM
Try me. I'm a captive audience.

     (XANDER stares at his sneakers.)

Okay. You're a captive audience. I'm not giving you a ride home until you talk to me.

     (XANDER's finger taps on his skull a few times. All his fingers drum on his scalp.
     He inhales deeply.)

                                XANDER
Remember when Kathy said that, in your day, there were men, women, and David Bowie?

                                 JIM
No, but go on.

                                XANDER
Well, when it comes to sexual orientation, I'm like David Bowie.

     (XANDER continues staring at his feet. A full thirty seconds pass. JIM shifts heavily
     on the concrete step, coming a bit closer and lowering his voice.)

                                 JIM
So you like guys. You're gay.

     (His voice rises unnaturally on the last word)

                                XANDER
I'm bisexual. I am sexually attracted to both men and women. I don't expect you to
condone it.

     (Brief silence)

                                JIM
How can I condone something I don't understand?

     (Brief silence)

That wasn't rhetorical. Help me understand. Start by telling me when you made this decision.

                                XANDER
     (His head shakes in his hands)

It's not a concept you opt for and shape to your liking. It chooses you.

     (He rubs his eyes and resumes his position, head in hands.)

It's difficult to explain. We can't control who we're attracted to. You can't imagine being attracted to a man, right? (Pause) Well, I can't imagine not being attracted to some men. It's not something I control.

                                JIM
But most of the world sees that as wrong. I don't know how it can feel right.

                                XANDER
I don't see how you marrying Kathy ten months after Mom died could feel right. But I accept it.

                                JIM
So what you're saying is, you can't change who you are.

     (XANDER nods.)

Then you'll understand that I can't change who I am either. Do I understand guys who love guys? No. Does it give me the heebie jeebies to think about? Yeah. (Pause) But you're my son.

     (XANDER waits, and wheezes)

                                JIM
I love you. You know that.

     (Brief silence)

So, all the women you said you were dating—were any of those real?

                                XANDER
Yes. All those women were real. They were not mannequins or blow-up dolls.

     (JIM guffaws. XANDER raises his head and looks at JIM. He laughs, too.)

XANDER, Cont'd

And I did go out with Sunny. And Charley—I'm not sure where that stands now though. But not Jess. Never Jess. (Shudders)

JIM

Well, son, I mean this for real: I hope someday you love someone—anyone—the way I loved your mother. When Emma died, I felt like a huge part of me—all the good parts—got erased. I'd look in the mirror and didn't recognize who I saw without her looking over my shoulder. I wasn't the same without her. I hope you never go through that.

XANDER

Why don't you ever talk about her? It's like you expunged her from our lives and we weren't allowed to grieve. You even hijacked all the photos.

JIM

I couldn't look at them. I guess I should've left them up, but I didn't want you kids to suffer. Like I was suffering. I thought it was better for everyone to move on.

XANDER

I had to hide the one torn photo I had under my mattress, like Mom was contraband.

JIM

What do you want from me, Alex?

XANDER

(Hesitates; a raspy coughing fit buys him some time)

For starters, can you call me Xander? I know Mom liked Alex but it's not the name that connects us to her. I think she'd welcome me adapting my name to something that fits me better, just like she'd understand my sexual orientation.

JIM

(Eyes narrowing)

Okay. Xander.

XANDER

And—

JIM

There's more?

(XANDER freezes)

I'm kidding. Keep going.

XANDER

Can we talk about Mom on occasion? Maybe trade a story or two?

                                    JIM
Sure. As long as they're not about the damn trophies.

        (XANDER tenses, then realizes JIM is smiling)

                                  XANDER
                                 (Lightly)

Dad, you have to get over this trophy hang-up. First of all, participation trophies didn't start with my generation. The baby boomers started it. Second of all, research indicates they don't cause any undue harm.

        (JIM scoffs.)

Plus, I'll tell you a secret. I never cared about the trophies. They didn't make me feel special at all. But Mom loved them so much, I never had the heart to tell her I thought they were asinine.

        (JIM leans back to regard his son. Nods, smiles and leans back in. He wraps an arm
        around XANDER's shoulder and squeezes.)

                                    JIM
What's with the cough and the wheezing? You're not getting asthma like your mother I hope.

                                  XANDER
It's only a tear gas hangover.

                                    JIM
        (Stares for a second before rolling his eyes)

Whatever.

        (JIM removes his arm and stands. XANDER also stands. JIM pulls his car keys from
        his coat pocket.)

Wanna grab breakfast?

                                  XANDER
I'm exhausted. I need to shower and sleep. Maybe some other time.

        (JIM grunts, moves down the steps and exits.)

                                  XANDER
No, wait—let's do it now.

        (He runs after his father)

        (Blackout)   THE END

Barn and Cloud

Mark Clarke

Telling Stories

Stacey Bowerman

I know a man who never speaks
of angels or God. He tells his childhood
tales with a gentle, rolling tongue.

I choose my own emotions to match
his vivid scenes. Words drawn out of his belly,
he quickly repairs as if something too heavy
ruins the taste. He offers careful, contemplated
details and always smiles his grey-whickered lips.
I ask how it felt to be left alone,
that child small enough to wind through
narrow ditches alone and strong enough
to plant a flowering garden for survival.

He remembers, he says, plowing the garden's rows
with only a stick, the same stick he used
to tear the head off a stalking snake,
the stick he used to knock away midsummer's weeds
climbing higher than what I imagine were his
small, steady eyes. I ask how it felt
and he says he can only remember laughing;
I don't tell him I think he is a liar.

Sabbatical at My Mother's

Stacey Bowerman

I plan to use her hipbones as handles
and throw my weight upwards
back into her womb.

It is an awkward trip to take, but possible
because these same industrious legs belonged to a child
who pumped a swing high and hard.

High and hard from Virginia to Michigan
and back in an afternoon, visiting grandparents
and eating red berries at rest stops.

I will ask her to hold her breath
and open her legs until it burns,
then I can slip roughly through.

Serotonin will run steady in my veins,
numbing the careful mending of my backbone.
Curling around myself, time will slow and stall.

She may not want me there,
it will be uncomfortable for her,
but I can accept this.

I might nestle my chin on her bladder
with unbearable pressure, and my elbows and heels
will surely collide with a delicate pattern of ribs.
Only when I am rested and full again
will I turn towards home.
The trip will be so sweet and slow.

Her legs will fly open again,
straining from what she thinks are her bowels,
until she dilates fully around herself.

I ease myself through,
breathless and erect,
a fistful of mucous - my souvenir.

Mother's Child

Stacey Bowerman

My feet hesitate on the gravel drive
as if each step forward comes with the effort
of walking through suctioning sand.
My duty to deliver groceries to the sick,
or what we call Mother when no other words
can explain. Knocking on the twilight
faded front door, waiting with only the sound
of my own noise answering back - I race through the
possibilities of careless accidents, a walk gone wrong,
or even the engineering of something larger.
Slowly a knot has drawn my stomach so far inward,
the pain seems lost in an oppressive coat of skin.
Still, no answer or maybe she hears only her inside
world where her child loses to God and his
endless demands. I step backwards on a frosty lawn
until the view allows the larger clue of a shadeless window -
a single light washes through the front room.
The scene reveals overflowing ashtrays and a bare mattress,
the only evidence of her life. A door opens into a hallway
fed solely by the room's glow, it is here a closer look
catches jerky movements reflected on a narrow section of wall.
Misshapen yet full of intent, flinging arms resemble a child's
shadow puppet. The figure moves as only a silhouette of
black - a shuffling-foot story. She plays out her drama alone
while I watch as a spectator drawn to others' tragedy
with a strangely eager eye - wondering if it is only her
God that despises me. Stepping away, gently
placing the groceries at her door -
I arrange them in precious circles of fruit
and towers of cans, a sacrifice at her altar.

Magic Bus

Mark Clarke

PICK UP AND GO ON
A one-act play with three scenes

Peter J. Grady

SYNOPSIS

A young female teenager enters a confessional at a Catholic Church and tells the priest that she is pregnant and has decided to seek an abortion. The priest tries to dissuade her. She ultimately reveals to him that she has learned he is her father. The teenager was conceived toward the end of his senior year in college. The priest does not believe her but ultimately is convinced that she is, indeed, his daughter. She requests his assistance—money—so she can leave the state to obtain a legal abortion. The scene shifts to a kitchen later that day, where the teenager tells her mother—a police officer—that she has found and confronted her father. Unlike her conversation with the priest, the teenager does not tell her mother that she is pregnant. The third scene occurs the next month. The priest is back at the church. The teenager's mother arrives. She orders the priest to have no contact with her daughter, unless she initiates the contact. The mother does not know and does not learn that her daughter was pregnant.

CHARACTERS

    PRIEST/THOMAS—a middle aged man, 35-45
    TEENAGER/AISHA—female, a recent high school graduate, 17-19
    GRACE/POLICE OFFICER—middle aged woman, 35-45
        (If possible, there should be a resemblance between Aisha and Grace or between Aisha and Thomas)

SETTING

    Time--summer, Saturday at noon, in a medium size American Midwest city
    SCENE I—the "confessional" in a Catholic Church
    SCENE 2—a kitchen, the same day
    SCENE 3—outside the "confessional", one month later

AT RISE

    The stage has two simple sets which sit side by side. Each set is lit only when in use. The SR set (SCENES 1 and 3) is a "box" in a church—a confessional with two compartments. The SL compartment of the box has a chair; the SR one has a kneeler. While in the confessional, actors face each other, but cannot see each other. The box is cut away so the audience can see the actors. The SL set (SCENE 2) is a simple kitchen—a small table with chairs with maybe coffee cups or a milk carton on the table. The play opens with a church bell tolling 12 times during which the curtain rises.

SCENE I

PRIEST appears SR, a folded newspaper under his arm. He is in black with a Roman collar. PRIEST glances at his wrist watch, makes a quick Sign of the Cross, closes his eyes, and while standing, prays silently. When he ends his prayer he makes another Sign of the Cross and looks around. There is no one else in the church. He looks at his watch again. Waits. Nothing. He picks up a bulletin.

PRIEST

(Reading aloud.)

"CONFESSIONS: EVERY SATURDAY AT NOON." If some sinners don't show up soon, I should have the entire hour to catch up on my reading.

(He looks at his watch again, shrugs, and goes to the SL confessional compartment and begins to read his paper. TEENAGER appears upstage in the church. She moves toward the confessional and then stops, reconsiders, and retreats back upstage into darkness. PRIEST hears her movement.)

PRIEST

Is someone there?

(He looks out, sees no one, and resumes reading. TEENAGER returns, pauses, and enters the confessional. She clears her throat. PRIEST continues reading. Finally, she knocks very loudly on the confessional wall. He puts down his paper.)

PRIEST

Hello? Is someone there?

TEENAGER

Yes. I am.

PRIEST

Oh, I'm sorry. Please forgive me. I thought I was alone. I don't usually get much business on Saturdays, so I was lost in my reading.

TEENAGER

Business?

PRIEST

Yes, you know. Confessions. Not many people come to Confession any more, so I wasn't expecting anyone. I am sorry I made you wait. You may begin.

(TEENAGER does not speak. There is a long pause.)

Um...can I help you?

TEENAGER

I don't know.

PRIEST

You don't know?

TEENAGER

I mean, I'm not sure why I'm here. Do I have to confess to be here?

PRIEST

Well, usually people come here because they have something to confess. They are seeking forgiveness. But sometimes people have something that they need to talk about.

TEENAGER

Maybe that's it. I have something I would like to talk about.

PRIEST

OK. You talk. I will listen.

TEENAGER

But first—how old are you?

PRIEST

What? Did you just ask my age?

TEENAGER

I heard that you are a "new" priest. I want to know how old you are.

PRIEST

Oh. People say I am a "new" priest because I haven't been at this parish or in this city for very long. I was transferred here about six months ago. But I have been ordained for 14 years.

TEENAGER

So you have only been out of college for...about 14 years?

PRIEST

No. Eighteen years. Four years of seminary in college. Four years of study in Rome. And then ordination.

TEENAGER

So that makes you...

PRIEST

An old man. I'm 40. Why?

TEENAGER

Just curious. A priest for 14 years and just transferred here? Why?

PRIEST

Wait—don't start. (A touch of anger) I work for the bishop, and he transfers priests whenever and wherever he wants. So NO—I was *not* transferred here because I abused someone at a former parish! (He pauses.)

TEENAGER

I didn't mean to imply anything…

PRIEST

I'm sorry. I get angry when I think about it. Some priests have committed many crimes over the years, and many of those crimes were hidden by transferring priests to different parishes. If it had happened only once it would be horrific, but there have been many victims. So much pain has been caused. I'm sorry. I get angry. And I am angry that the sight of my collar triggers fear and hatred for so many people.

TEENAGER

The sight of your collar? The Roman collar priests wear?

PRIEST

That we *sometimes* wear. I don't wear it when I am shopping or otherwise in public. I was once assaulted because I was wearing a collar. By the victim of a priest.

TEENAGER

You have been attacked? For wearing a collar?

PRIEST

Yes—for the sins of one of my brethren. I can't really blame the man who attacked me. He had been horribly abused. But that made me stop wearing the collar when I am out in public.

TEENAGER

I did not mean to offend or imply anything. I really don't care why you were transferred here. All I really wanted to know was your age. Oh, and your name. I don't go to church here. What is your name?

PRIEST

Well, most people call me "Father Kelly"…

TEENAGER

(sharply)

I do not want to call you "Father." What is your name?

PRIEST

(taken aback)

Oh? Well, my name is Thomas.

TEENAGER

Thomas Kelly?

PRIEST

Most people call me "Father Kelly". But my friends call me "Thomas."

TEENAGER

Oh. *(Pause.)* I'm sorry I asked for your name, because I am not going to tell you my name.

PRIEST

There is no need for names. Confession is confidential. God knows who you are. I don't need to know. But I would like to know why you are here. Do you wish to confess? Or just talk?

TEENAGER
(suddenly upset)
Neither. This was a stupid idea. I'm sorry I bothered you. *(She stands.)* I'm in the wrong place anyway. Good bye.

(She begins to leave.)

PRIEST

Wait! Hey! Wait...calm down. This might be the right place. We can "just talk." Are you alright? (She reconsiders; does not leave the confessional)... Okay. Feeling better? Great. So! Let's talk. What's on your mind?

TEENAGER

I'm pregnant. (Pause)

PRIEST

And...?

TEENAGER

And I'm not married, and I am not going to marry... .

PRIEST

I see. Well, it is not the end of the world. The Church offers help and support, and...

TEENAGER

And I'm going to get an abortion.

(PRIEST is silent. She repeats, louder this time.)

I said, "I am going to get an abortion."

PRIEST

And...you want me to say...what? What do you expect me to say?

TEENAGER

I don't know what to expect. But I want to know what you think.

PRIEST

You know what the Church thinks. That abortion is wrong. That abortion destroys a life. That it scars your soul. That the whole idea of abortion demeans civilization. That having an abortion will be a burden for the rest of your life.

TEENAGER

But what do *you* think?

PRIEST

I think...I think that you still haven't decided whether to seek an abortion. I think you still have a big decision to make. And I want to encourage you to have the baby. But I *think* that no matter what I say, you are the person who must decide. (A pause) I *hope* and *will pray* that you have the baby.

TEENAGER

Encourage me? I'm sorry, but I can't see any other way. And besides, it is my choice.

PRIEST

I know. It is your choice. But there are right choices and wrong choices...

TEENAGER

(interrupts*)*

And some choices are right for some people and not right for others. But I am old enough to know that there are no easy choices. Whatever I choose, I will live with.

PRIEST

Important choices are never easy... . We think on them; we pray on them; we decide, and then we go forward. And then we live with the consequences. And *you* will live with the consequences of this decision.

TEENAGER

NO! Don't start with the guilt trip. I can guess what you are about to say—"What if your mother had made the choice you are considering?"

PRIEST

No. No guilt trip. You asked what I think, and I told you. And now I am simply acknowledging that the choice will not be easy. And I am advising you to think long and hard before choosing. Pray long and hard before choosing. And know that you will live with the consequences of your choice. For whatever you choose, there will be consequences. (Silence.) Are you really willing to talk with me about this?

TEENAGER

I think so.

                              PRIEST
Have you talked with your mother about this?

                             TEENAGER
Of course.

        (Pause. She decides to tell the truth.)

Actually, no, I haven't. I decided I won't tell her. I've been a burden to her for my whole
life, and she doesn't need me to give her another thing to worry about. I must decide this
myself. She has worried about me for too many years already. But I need to talk with
someone… . I'm probably in the wrong place—I haven't been to Confession since Middle
School. I don't even know what to say. *(Pause.)* But here I am.

                              PRIEST
And you are welcome here.

                             TEENAGER
But this won't make any difference. I have made up my mind, and I am getting the
abortion.

                              PRIEST
Have you talked with your father?

                             TEENAGER
                          (a flash of anger)
I never knew my father. He doesn't even know he *is* a father. My mother says he never
knew. If I find him, I will ask for help—but I need to be certain that I find him.

                              PRIEST
What kind of help would you ask of him?

                             TEENAGER
I need money.

                              PRIEST
Money?

                             TEENAGER
I need money. I can't get an abortion here anymore. I am too far along. I have to go
somewhere else.

                              PRIEST
Where do you need to go?

                             TEENAGER
I don't know yet. Some place other than here--some different state—a state where I can
actually get an abortion and where I can afford the cost of an airplane ticket and a ride to a

cheap hotel. Even if I make it to one of those states where I can still get an abortion, I will need to sit through a waiting period. I need money to go somewhere, and I need...

PRIEST

You need money, and you need time to think and pray. I won't give you money. But you *must* take the time to think. And pray. Talk to your mother. Talk to the father of the child.

TEENAGER

There is no "father" because there is no "child". There is a fetus. It is growing. And there is no time to think. In this state, I am already too far along to get an abortion.

PRIEST

Then I can't help you, even if I wanted—which I do NOT. If I gave you money to help you get an abortion, I would be committing a crime. And more importantly, I would be committing a grievous sin.

TEENAGER

I knew you would say that.

PRIEST

Then why did you come here? You don't want to talk about this. You have already made your decision, and now all you want is money. Did you really think you would get it here? Here in the church? From me, a priest? If this is your idea of a joke—it is not funny. You need to leave. Right now.

TEENAGER

I will not leave. This is not a joke.

PRIEST

Then what the hell is it?

TEENAGER

I believe it is the first meeting between me and my biological father.

PRIEST

What?!?

TEENAGER

I believe you are my biological father. And this is the first time I have met you.

PRIEST

What?!? This is insane! You are insane!

TEENAGER

I am not insane. You are, biologically, my father. I have never seen you before, and you probably didn't know I existed. (Pause) You dated my mother in college. Your sperm impregnated her. You are, technically, my "father", Father. And I need your help.

PRIEST

(Exploding with anger)

This isn't possible! I don't know what you are talking about. You need to leave.

TEENAGER

Your senior year of college—you met, and dated, and impregnated—a woman named
Grace. I hope you loved her, because I am her daughter.

PRIEST

You are pretty young for extortion, young lady. If this was not the confessional, I would call
the cops. For now—I am asking you to leave. If you will not, I will call the police.

(She does not move from her place in the confessional.)

You must leave now!

(He gets up—leaves the confessional. She does not move.)

(Looks around the church and then at his watch; announces)

It is one o'clock. Confessions are over. The church is closed for the remainder of the
day...And you will be leaving right now.

(He goes to the confessional, reaches in, and grabs her by the arm and pulls her out
of the confessional. They struggle. He looks at her for the first time and stops.)

Oh...!

TEENAGER

This is not extortion. This is your past. This is the truth. You are the man who got my
mother pregnant.

PRIEST

Your mother?

TEENAGER

Yes. My mother. I just put it all together two or three days ago, and I have been debating
what to say or do about it ever since. And then, yesterday after work, I stopped at the
drugstore and bought a pregnancy test. And now I know I have no time to discuss this or to
debate you. I am pregnant. You are my biological father. I want an abortion, and I can't
afford one. And I want you to pay for it.

PRIEST

Your mother is...Grace?

TEENAGER

Yes.

PRIEST

Did she put you up to this? Did she say I would pay for an abortion—an abortion of my...my grandchild?

TEENAGER

(Strong—defends her mother)

I already told you--my mother does not know that I am pregnant. And she doesn't know I am here. And she doesn't know that *I* know who you are.

PRIEST

But...

TEENAGER

And you do not have a "grandchild"—you have a biological daughter who does not want to be here, but who needs your help. (Long pause.) You have nothing to say?

PRIEST

Please. Let me think a moment.

(They look at one another.)

TEENAGER

I've always wondered... . I've only seen one photo...

PRIEST

I didn't even wonder...I think I can see Grace...a memory of Grace. That brief smile. (Pause) But no! No! This cannot be true. I never even conceived of something like this—

TEENAGER

"Conceived"? That's an interesting choice of words.

PRIEST

(Flustered) I mean I never...dreamed...

TEENAGER

You did not know? You are serious?

PRIEST

I did not know. I didn't even suspect anything.

TEENAGER

Well, something happened! Tell me! I am here, and you are my father. Something happened!

PRIEST

I'm sorry. I can't. I don't know. For God's sake, ask your mother! Ask...Grace.

TEENAGER

I have been asking her since I was old enough to talk—begging her for details. And I just figured this out this week. She has told me nothing—I had to find out on my own.

PRIEST

She told you...

TEENAGER

Nothing about you—no real facts about you. Nothing except vague stories. Not even your real name. When I would ask what happened to you, she said that you had been killed in a car accident before I was born.

PRIEST

I died in a car accident?

TEENAGER

(Nods) She said that she loved you. And she said that you loved her.

PRIEST

I did. I loved her. I mean, I loved *Grace*. But are you Grace's daughter? You know nothing about me, and I know nothing about you. No! You are not Grace's daughter. And I am not your father. (Rising anger) You show up here with no warning. You tell me you are my daughter. You tell me that you are pregnant, you plan to have an abortion, and you expect me to pay for it. That sounds like extortion to me, young lady.

TEENAGER

My mother said that she loved you. And she said that you loved her.

PRIEST

I loved...Grace.

TEENAGER

You loved her so much that you left her—you disappeared from her life?

PRIEST

That is not fair. I *loved Grace*. Grace never told me she was pregnant. *She* disappeared. I did not disappear—she always knew where I was, what I was, and what I wanted to be—a priest.

TEENAGER

Tell me the details.

PRIEST

No. Ask your mother. Ask Grace if she really is your mother.

TEENAGER

She has told me nothing except lies. Tell me the truth.

PRIEST

You are persistent. Like Grace.

TEENAGER

I have no choice. I have no time. Tell me.

PRIEST
(Relenting)

Tell *me* something first. What is your name? What is my daughter's name?

TEENAGER

Aisha.

PRIEST
(He chuckles.)

Aisha? Well....you convinced me of one thing. Your name tells me everything. You are Grace's daughter.

TEENAGE GIRL/AISHA

My name tells you everything? It tells me nothing! She never explained why she chose my name...

PRIEST

I can explain. I met Grace on the first day of my last semester, my senior year of college. We had a history class together—The Modern Middle East. I had to take it for my major in theology because it was the only class at school that had anything to do with Islam.

AISHA

And my name?

PRIEST

"Aisha" was one of the Prophet Mohammed's wives.

AISHA

I know she was one of his wives. I know how to use Wikipedia. And I know that she "was highly regarded for her intellect and knowledge in various fields, including poetry and medicine." But Wikipedia doesn't tell me *why* I was named for her.

PRIEST

You were named Aisha because Grace asked a question in class, and the professor didn't know the answer.

AISHA

And what does that...?

PRIEST

Grace asked about the Prophet's wives, and the professor did not have a clue—not only was he not able to tell her anything about the Prophet's wives, he didn't even know the Prophet had been married more than once. Grace pointed out that there was a whole chapter on the

PRIEST, Cont'd

wives in the textbook, and then asked why we students had spent over $100 for the book *he* required for the course when he didn't even know what was in the book.

AISHA

That sounds like my mother.

PRIEST

Yes—she made a lot of sense! So, we became friends.

AISHA

And so…

PRIEST

And so we began to date. And considered ourselves a couple—she was my "girlfriend," and I was her "boyfriend"—and we dated until I graduated. We teased each other about her question. We said that, if we ever were married and had a daughter, we would name her "Aisha"—because it is a beautiful name. Which was crazy—because we knew we were never going to be married.

AISHA

How did you know that?

PRIEST

Because I was in the seminary. Because I was going to be a priest. We both knew that—we knew our time together was not real. Almost like a vacation. We knew it would end.

AISHA

And it ended?

PRIEST

Yes. It ended.

AISHA

How? And why?

PRIEST

The "why" is easy. I was going to Rome to complete my studies to be ordained a priest. We both knew that. But the "how"?

(He shakes his head; Aisha encourages him to continue.)

After graduation I went to visit my brother and his family in Canada—he couldn't make it to my graduation—but Grace and I had made plans to get back together when I returned. We had the whole summer ahead of us before I had to be in Rome and so…

AISHA

So…?

84

PRIEST

While in Canada I tried to call her, but I got no answer. After a couple of days, I called again and got a recording which said that the number had been disconnected. I called a friend, who said he hadn't seen her. When I got back to town, she was gone. No forwarding address. No note. No nothing. Not even a family member to contact. I haven't seen her since.

AISHA

Did you try to find her?

PRIEST

Of course. But everything was a dead end. All I ever knew about her as that she was an only child. An Air Force brat—had lived all over and gone to ten different schools. Her dad was a mechanic. A lifer. He died a month before she entered college. He was apparently quite skillful and was in great demand—the Air Force would send him around the country to train other mechanics.

AISHA

And her mother?

PRIEST

She wouldn't talk about her mother, except to say that her mom had died when she was a baby. No other family. No real hometown. I tried... . I have typed her name into many, many search engines. I have never found any reference to her—to her name—or to any clue which would allow me to find her. She disappeared.

AISHA

And you didn't know she was pregnant?

PRIEST

No! God no! If I had known that...

AISHA

What? What would have you done if you had known that?

PRIEST

....I don't know...

AISHA

You don't know?

PRIEST

No. I *did not* know she was pregnant, and so I don't know what I would have done. I *think* I would have asked Grace to marry me. I *think* I would have said good-bye to ever becoming a priest. But I don't know what I would have done. And more importantly, I don't know what would have happened.

AISHA

That is the second time you've said that.

PRIEST

Because I don't know. What would Grace have decided? Perhaps together we would have decided to get married. Or she might have decided to get an abortion and not tell me about it. Or she could have decided to get an abortion and tell me about it—and I don't know if I would have supported that decision or not. But abortion was her decision, not mine. And because I knew nothing, I wasn't even able to have a discussion about it.

AISHA

It was her decision. You said earlier that this was my decision. Did you mean that?

PRIEST

Yes.

AISHA

You hypocrite. Ten minutes ago you said "abortion is wrong". That it "destroys a life, that it scars your soul," and that an abortion will be "a burden" for the rest of my life.

PRIEST

That is what the Church thinks. And I think it is a part of my job to tell you and everyone else what the Church thinks.

AISHA

And so every year, right before the fall elections, you and every other preacher rants and raves about abortion—telling everyone to vote for the so-called "pro life" candidates.

PRIEST

The Church has designated the month of October as "pro-life" month. I preach about abortion every year, whether it is an election year or not—but I also talk about the death penalty, a need to control guns, a need to show compassion, a need to support immigrants...

AISHA

But when there is an election, you talk abortion, every Sunday in October and for good measure, the first Sunday in November—two days before election day. A person can't get in or out of the church without being given a leaflet with pictures of babies—some alive, and some horribly mangled—to drive home your point. You are actually telling the congregation, "Vote for *this* candidate. Vote for *this* party. The other candidates and the other party just want to kill babies."

PRIEST

I have never condoned that electioneering outside the church.

AISHA

And you have done nothing to stop it, either. And anyone listening to your sermons could tell who you are endorsing.

PRIEST

I have never endorsed any candidate or party from the pulpit!

AISHA

Give me a break! Give the people in the pews a break! They know. They hear you and know exactly what you are saying. So tell me again—make me believe what you really think. You said that whether to have an abortion was my mother's decision—and only her decision. Did you mean that?

PRIEST

It was her decision. No matter my thoughts or feelings were or would have been, the decision was hers to make.

AISHA

And so you meant that when you said this decision was only mine to make?

PRIEST

Yes.

AISHA

But what do you *think* about the decision?

PRIEST

I think…I think that you still haven't decided whether to seek an abortion. I think you still have a big decision to make. I can tell you what I think, but I can't—and won't—presume to tell you what to do. I want to encourage you to allow the pregnancy to go on—to have a baby. But I *think* that no matter what I say, you are the person who must decide. (A pause) As I said before, I *hope* and *will pray* that you have the baby. The decision is yours. Yours alone.

AISHA

Only it *isn't* my decision anymore. The state has decided that for me. I calculated the earliest I could have gotten pregnant—and if I am correct, then *even though I just found out today,* I am already too far along for an abortion—at least here, in this state. Our state law says I am already one week past what state law allows. Abortion is no longer a choice for me. Now it is a crime—a crime for me and for anyone who helps me get an abortion, in this state or in another state.

PRIEST

A crime? It would be a crime?

AISHA

You haven't been paying attention, have you? In this state, to abort this fetus now I would be committing a crime. I can't go to a clinic here. All of the clinics have been shut down. The new law says that I and everyone else involved would be committing a crime. And, if anyone helps me get an abortion, or helps me go out of state to get an abortion—

PRIEST

So if I gave you money to leave the state to go somewhere you could legally obtain an abortion, I would be guilty of a crime too?

AISHA

The only chance I have for a safe abortion is a plane ticket out of state. And I, and anyone who helps me get that ticket will commit a crime in this state. If I stay here...If I stay here, in this state, the only choice I have for an abortion is a coat hanger.

PRIEST

Oh God, no!

AISHA

I am here to ask for money. I need plane fare. I need cash for a hotel and food.

PRIEST

And you need to pay the clinic and the doctor who performs the abortion. You will need...you will need several thousand dollars!

AISHA

Yes, I guess so...and I have to...I have to. (She begins to sob.) Dammit! I have to do everything. There is too much. I need to take time off from work without getting fired. Dammit!

PRIEST

I think you need to tell your mother. You need to tell Grace.

AISHA

NO! That is the last thing I can do. She can't find out...

PRIEST

Why?

AISHA

Because she is a cop. She will have to arrest me if she finds out. If she doesn't arrest me, and anyone finds out, she will be fired, will lose her career, and probably end up in jail. She has spent her entire life protecting me. Supporting me. Helping me. Loving me! She is proud of the career she has built in law enforcement. But you—my father—you have done nothing for me. I am your daughter. I am asking you for one thing. Only one thing. Money.

PRIEST

And what of *my* career?

AISHA

I don't give a damn about your career. The only thing that is important to me about *your* career is that you can't repeat what I have told you. Confession has its benefits after all. (PRIEST starts to protest; she shuts him down.) I am your daughter. You have never done anything to deserve the name "father" to me, but I am asking you now: You are my father, and I need your help.

PRIEST

Then ask the father of the child!

                                  AISHA

NO!

                                  PRIEST

Why? He is as responsible as you...

                                  AISHA

He is more responsible. He said he was wearing a rubber. He is a liar and an idiot, and he
probably would report me to the cops if he found out.

                                  PRIEST

And if I do not help? You will expose me? You will go to the newspaper?

                                  AISHA

No. This is not extortion. This is a request. I have made my decision, and I have made my
request. If you will not help me, I will do what I can to find the money. There are men who
would pay to spend time with me. I don't want to do that, but I will if I must. And if I can't
raise the money, I will find a coat hanger. I have made my decision. You need to make
yours.

                                  PRIEST

Do you think I have thousands of dollars I can just hand over to you?

                                  AISHA

I don't know. But you could borrow it. You could walk into your bank on Monday morning
and borrow the money without having to explain anything to anybody. I can't do that.
Please. I need the money. And I need it soon.

                                  PRIEST

I need...to think. And pray. We need to meet again. I know—soon. (Silence, as he
considers.) I don't know if I can get the money. I don't know if I should get the money.
But...I need to think. Call me tomorrow afternoon. After Mass. Do not call the rectory.
Here. (Hands her a business card). My cell phone number. I need to think. Then we can
talk.

SCENE 2

        Later that day. Kitchen set on SL as described above. GRACE is seated at the table,
        drinking coffee, and reading the paper. She has just gotten off work—she is a police
        officer. Her uniform jacket is hanging on a chair. AISHA enters SL, dressed as she
        was in SCENE I. She approaches GRACE and gives her a perfunctory kiss.

                                  GRACE

Hi, honey. You were up and out early—you're all dressed up. Where to on a Saturday?

                                  AISHA

Just had some things to do before the day got away from me.

(AISHA motions to GRACE's uniform jacket.)

What about you? Didn't you work third shift? I thought you'd still be in bed.

GRACE

I just got home a minute ago. Two split shifts today. I have to go back this evening.
Mandatory overtime tonight. There's a protest march at City Hall starting at 7:00.

AISHA

Who is protesting and for what?

GRACE

Not really sure—I think all I have to do tonight will be traffic control. Boring, but the
overtime is nice. I did some traffic work this morning and after I get some sleep, I will
spend a couple of hours down at City Hall this evening. We can use the overtime money for
your tuition and books this fall.

AISHA

Yeah. Time for me to start to worry about money.

GRACE

(Resumes reading her paper.)

I'm not worried about tuition! But I don't want to take out a mortgage for your *books*!

AISHA

Books are *that* expensive? Hmmmm. (Pours herself a cup of coffee.) Mom...can we talk
about my father...again?

GRACE

(Sighs)

Again? (Pause.) Aisha, your father died before you were born. A car crash. We have talked
about this many times.

AISHA

I know. And every time I ask, you say the same thing. "Your father was a man named
Thomas Bennett who died in a car crash."

GRACE

You saw his grave, Aisha. Remember, when you started Middle School, you insisted on
seeing his grave, so we drove clear across the state to look at the grave...

AISHA
(Interrupting)
And in a beautiful country cemetery we saw *a* grave. We saw a grave with a tombstone. And
the name "Thomas Bennett" was on the tombstone.

GRACE

What are you saying, Aisha?

AISHA

That I went back to the cemetery, Mom—over Spring Break.

GRACE

You told me you were going to a concert over Spring Break.

AISHA

I lied.

    (GRACE lowers her paper to speak but Aisha speaks over her.)

I LIED, Mom! Just as you have lied to me all of these years. I went back to the cemetery, and I found the grave, and then I spent the afternoon in the local library. I read the city newspapers in the archives, and I found out about "Thomas Bennett."

GRACE

What are you saying?

AISHA

There *is* a man named Thomas Bennett buried in that cemetery, Mom. But "Thomas Bennett" died in a farm accident. He was caught in a grain bin and suffocated. And he never went to college.

GRACE

Your father died in a car crash…

AISHA

No. I read the story, Mom. I saw the obituary.

    (GRACE is silent.)

I'm not sure I *ever* believed you, Mom. Your story never made sense… .

GRACE

Car crashes never make sense. I know this. I'm a cop, remember? Car crashes happen because somebody was stupid or drunk or just plain unlucky. They happen. And when they happen, you have to pick up and move on.

AISHA

Or when you get pregnant and don't get married, you pick up and move on…and then you lie and hope that your child will never know the truth.

GRACE

I hope I have heard the word "lie" come out of your mouth for the *last* time.

AISHA
(Accusatory)

Your story never made sense. You never talked about his parents—*my* grandparents. I had no family! I not only had no father, I had no aunts or uncles or grandparents. And there were no newspaper articles about the car crash. No photos of my father to look at.

GRACE

I burned…

AISHA

I've heard your story before—too many times. You told me you were so upset that you burned the only photos you had of him… .

GRACE

I was upset…

AISHA

I am sure you were upset about what happened. And you probably did burn any photos you had of him…But did you burn every article about the crash in every newspaper in the state? Did you burn the death certificate? Did you?

GRACE

I don't want to talk about this. I told you what happened. I was in love. I got pregnant. He died in a car crash. The end.

AISHA
(Patiently)

Mom, for the past year I have been spending hours on the internet trying to find some answers. I have been going to every library I could think of, trying to find old newspaper stories that reported the crash. I looked at every obituary I could find for every young man who died, from a year before my birth to a year after. I have been to three different courthouses, and I even wrote to the Secretary of State, looking for a death certificate for a "Thomas Bennett"—but there are no records for "Thomas Bennett" except for the man who suffocated in the grain bin—the man who is buried in that beautiful cemetery we went to. But, Mom, there are no records of a car crash! No records anywhere. None! Because *your* "Thomas Bennett who died in a car crash" *never existed.*

(GRACE is silent. AISHA becomes quieter.)

But I found a college yearbook in your dresser the day before yesterday…your "one semester" college where you said my father was a senior. The yearbook for the year before I was born.

GRACE
(Suddenly outraged)

What were you doing in my dresser? That is my private…

                              AISHA
                        (Speaking over Grace)
I found the yearbook and, in the yearbook, there was only one senior named "Thomas".
Only one "Thomas." But his name was not "Thomas Bennett."

                              GRACE
I don't have to listen to this.

                              AISHA
Only one senior named "Thomas." His last name was "Kelly." Don't lie to me anymore,
Mom.

        (GRACE protests, but AISHA speaks over her.)

And "Thomas Kelly" was a seminarian. A seminarian, Mom! Thomas Kelly. He was a
seminarian then. He did not die. And now he is a priest.

                              GRACE
Why are you doing this to me?

                              AISHA
Why have you been lying to me my entire life? My father did not die—and you knew he was
alive, and you knew he became a priest! But you lied to me! Why, Mom? WHY?...Why?

                              GRACE
I am not going to talk about this.

                              AISHA
You ARE going to talk about it. You owe me that, dammit!

                              GRACE
I owe you nothing. I have given you everything...always...and everything I have is yours.
You have no right...

        (She looks at AISHA and stops.)

Yes, I suppose now that you do have a right. You are 18 years old. I owe you the truth.

                              AISHA
Finally.

                              GRACE
Finally? Yes...I lied. I lied because I made the best choice I could at the time. I made a
choice. And I didn't look back.

                              AISHA
You chose...?

GRACE

I chose to become a mother, Aisha. A *single* mother. I chose to start over—to become a mother. I chose to change my name, and I chose to disappear. Because I did not want him to find me. Or to find you.

AISHA

Just like that?

GRACE

Of course, not "just like that." Don't trivialize this, Aisha. I planned. I changed my name. I worked to become a new person.

AISHA

   (Pause)

Did you think about abortion?

GRACE

Of course! I had to think about it. It was a real possibility—back then...I had my whole future ahead of me...and he—Thomas—would not even talk about marriage, or of living together. He had one goal—to become a priest.

AISHA

Didn't you even tell him...?

GRACE:

No. He never knew that I was pregnant—but I knew that he had his whole 'priestly' life planned out. So I had to make some decisions.

AISHA

And you thought...

GRACE

I thought about everything. So, of course, I thought about abortion. And..after thinking long and hard, I chose to have the baby. To have you.

AISHA

But if you had aborted me, you could have gone on—you could have gotten your college degree.

GRACE

But I wouldn't have had you, and the life we have had together. I know. If I had gotten an abortion...everything would have been different. But...But I didn't make that choice. I chose to have a baby, and that baby turned out to be you. And then, when you were old enough to ask, I chose to pretend that your father was dead... I made choices.

   (She is suddenly irritated.)

And don't patronize me. There is nothing wrong with my law enforcement degree. I am proud that I went to the Academy, and I am proud that I have been a cop for 15 years.

AISHA

But...

GRACE

No buts. I thought it through, and I made my decision. And together you and I have lived with the consequences of that decision. That choice. And Aisha, if I had made a different choice, I would have lived with *those* consequences.

AISHA

But...

GRACE
(forcefully)

"But"? I have no time for "buts". This is what happens when a person grows up. Life happens to you and you have to decide, and then you have to live with your decisions.

AISHA

Do you ever regret...?

GRACE

Of course, I don't regret. And. of course, I *do* regret. I regret the life I didn't have. The life I could have had. And I regret not telling you the truth about your father. And I *don't* regret lying to you about your father. And I argue with myself and sometimes I am right and sometimes I am wrong...But no matter what, I have to go back to work tonight at 7:00 o'clock, and I will make some extra overtime money and that will come in handy. Because the choices that I made put us here—both of us—and gave us all the problems and all the promises we have together. And so we pick up and go on.

AISHA

But what if...?

GRACE

It didn't happen. *You* happened.

AISHA

How long did it take you to decide?

GRACE

I don't know—two or three weeks after I learned I was pregnant. I know that when I finally decided, I still would have been able to have received an abortion. Not like now—some states deny all abortions no matter how long a woman has been pregnant. Like our state— our governor and legislature are going crazy—yesterday the governor had a press conference and talked about setting up special investigative units to find and prosecute anyone who provides or receives an abortion. And a couple of the cops down at the station want to volunteer! Goddamn idiots.

AISHA

A special unit? What are they going to do? Stake out doctor's clinics? Do undercover work at drugstores to see who is buying pregnancy test kits?

GRACE

I don't know. This is crazy. I can't believe that I might be ordered to serve an arrest warrant on a woman who got an abortion—which is every woman's right! I was born at the right time. I was one of the lucky ones—I had a chance to think things through. Women today—girls like you—are being told what to do and threatened with jail.

AISHA

So you thought about having an abortion? You could have had one, but…

GRACE

It didn't happen. I decided against it. *You* happened.

AISHA

But why the story about my father? Why the lies? Why the goddamn car crash and the fake name and everything else?

GRACE

Why? So you would never find out. So we would never have this talk. So you would never find out that I changed my name, so he couldn't find me. So you would never go looking for a father who didn't exist…for a "father" who couldn't be your father and who didn't even know you existed.

AISHA

But why *not* an abortion? I need to know, Mom.

GRACE

I don't know. I thought about abortion. I knew it was a choice, and it was probably the only wise choice…

AISHA

But you didn't make that choice. Why?

GRACE

In the final analysis, Aisha, the *why* is none of your business. That was *my* choice. And I do not have to explain it or justify it, to you or to anyone else. No woman should ever have to explain that to anyone. I decided. I made the decision to have you. And I have never looked back.

AISHA

Never regretted?

GRACE

I didn't say that, and I won't say that. I told you that I carry around some regret. I have some regret—regret for me, and for the life I have.

(AISHA expected a different answer).

GRACE, Cont'd

Honey, I made a choice and I lived with it. It's like when I decided to become a cop. I thought about it, made my decision, and entered the Academy. Some days I think I must have been crazy to become a cop, and other days I can't imagine doing anything else. You make choices in life. You live with your choices. You pick up and go on and try to be happy. (Pause) I tried to make a good life for both of us.

AISHA

(Not yet ready to forgive)

And part of that "good life" was to lie to me about my father?

GRACE

(Steadily, unapologetic)

Yes. I lied about your father. And I changed my last name, so he could never find me, and I lied about his last name because I naively thought those two lies would make it impossible for you to find *him*.

AISHA

Do you know where he is now? Could you find him if you wanted to?

GRACE

I know where he is. He moved to town about a year ago. I have kept track of him. I saw him last week at the grocery store. He wasn't wearing his collar, but it was him. I don't think he saw me.

AISHA

He's the new priest, isn't he...Father Thomas Kelly. I met him today. I told him who I was.

(Silence—they stare at each other as the scene ends.)

SCENE 3

> One month later. The SR church set. PRIEST is seated in the Confessional, reading
> the paper. Otherwise, the church is empty. GRACE appears SR wearing her uniform.
> She waits quietly, her arms folded. After an overlong pause, PRIEST looks out and
> sees GRACE. He moves to greet her.

PRIEST

I thought I heard the door. I'm sorry. I hope you weren't waiting very long. How can I help
you, Officer? If you are here for confession, I am free right now. You won't even have to
take a number!

(GRACE does not move or respond. PRIEST stands up and walks toward her.)

Is something wrong, Officer?

GRACE

I am not here to confess, Thomas. (She gestures to his Roman collar.) I almost didn't
recognize you in your uniform! I guess my uniform has you confused too.

THOMAS

Do I know you?

GRACE

You could at least *pretend* to remember me.

THOMAS

Remember you? (He draws closer.) Oh my God! Grace!

(THOMAS moves to her, but her demeanor makes it clear this is not a friendly visit.
He takes a step back. They look at each other.)

It *is* you.

GRACE

Yes. It is me.

THOMAS

I don't know what to say. It is you. I tried to find you. I can't tell you how long I tried to
find you.

GRACE

Don't even try to tell me. I am not interested. You tried to find me and you failed. And I
tried to *hide you*—and I also failed.

THOMAS

You tried to *hide* me?

GRACE

Last month, you met a young woman here, and you told her about me.

THOMAS

Yes...of course. And more importantly, she told me about herself. And about you. And she told me she knew who I was. She said...she said you named her Aisha.

GRACE

Yes. I named her Aisha. She found you. You didn't find us.

THOMAS

I really don't care who found whom. *You are here!*

GRACE

I care because I wish I was *not* here. I did not want to find you, Thomas, and I did not *need* to find you. But you were found because I couldn't hide you anymore.

THOMAS

Grace, is this some kind of a game? A riddle? "I tried to find you. You tried to hide me." What do you mean?

GRACE

You know her name. Do you believe she is your daughter?

THOMAS

Yes. She convinced me—her name alone told was almost enough to convince me: *Aisha*, "who was highly regarded for her intellect and knowledge in various fields, including poetry and medicine..."

GRACE

I should have realized it would be a red flag...But I wanted a beautiful name for my daughter.

THOMAS

My daughter too. I found out from her...it would have been nice if you had told me.

GRACE

You were not told because you do *not* have a daughter. Aisha has found the man who biologically is her father.

THOMAS

You are playing with words...

GRACE

No. I am not playing with words. You do *not* have a daughter. You didn't know I was pregnant. You can't be responsible for something that you didn't know about.

THOMAS

That sounds like something I might say.

GRACE

Yes, I could hear you saying that. And you would add that it would be pretty stupid to think you were responsible for something you didn't know about. "Pretty stupid"—yes, I think that's what you would say. Well, Thomas, there was a time when we both were pretty stupid.

(Thomas begins to speak but she stops him.)

Thomas, don't let yourself think you have a daughter. You knew nothing about her, and you still know nothing about her. *She means nothing to you.* And I *wish* that you meant nothing to her. But she has been looking for you for years and, despite my best efforts, she found you.

THOMAS

And she told you she had found me.

GRACE

Yes. She told me.

THOMAS

When did she tell you?

GRACE

What? When did she tell me? She told me the day that she found you. But why does that matter?

THOMAS

You learned that she found me a month ago—and *now* you come to see me? Is she alright? Has something happened to her? Why did you wait, and why are you here now?

(He is concerned, and his voice becomes desperate.)

Is she alright? Has something happened?

GRACE

(Surprised at his tone.)

She is fine. She is home, living with me. Now, at any rate. We had a bit of a falling out, shortly after she found you. She got angry and decided she was going to move out— actually, she stormed out. She said she would move in with her boyfriend. And so I didn't see her for awhile...

THOMAS

But she returned?

GRACE

Yes. She was gone for awhile, but a week to ten days later, she returned. And things are going better now.

THOMAS

A falling out? What do you mean?

GRACE

She said she had to leave—that she couldn't stay with me anymore. That I was a liar and that I had made her life one big lie. So she blew up, packed a few things, and left.

THOMAS

Where did she go? Is she safe?

GRACE

She is 18 years old. She left, and she came back. Maybe she figured out that the boyfriend is an idiot—so it was a good thing. She seems happier now. She says she broke up with him.

THOMAS

So she is safe?

GRACE

She is safe. Am I supposed to be touched that you care enough to ask? You seem very concerned about someone who didn't even exist in your life a month ago.

THOMAS

I…I am just worried about her… . That is all. She is my daughter…

GRACE

No. She is *not* your daughter.

THOMAS

But…

GRACE

Get that out of your head. And by what right do you chastise me for "waiting a whole month" to see you?

THOMAS

I guess I thought…

GRACE

Why did I wait to come here? You really haven't changed, you know that? You are all upset because I didn't come running to see you! It has always been all about you, hasn't it, Thomas? And it still is.

(He starts to speak and she cuts him off.)

I didn't *want* to see you. Ever. When you chose the Church, I chose motherhood. I did not want to ever see you again.

THOMAS

And yet you are here…

GRACE

I am here, but only to tell you who she is.

THOMAS

Yes. Of course. Thank you. I am grateful that you…

GRACE

…and to tell you—to *order* you—to leave her alone.

THOMAS

Leave her alone? I have done nothing to contact her! But she found me! She found me! Are you "ordering" her to pretend that I do not exist? That badge and gun of yours has gone to your head, Grace. Please, fill me in, oh, mighty Officer—what should happen next in this little drama?

GRACE

She will decide what is next. *She* will decide whether and when to ever see you again.

THOMAS

But *you* came to see me. And I have a daughter…

GRACE

I came to see you because I owed you an explanation. But *you* do not have a daughter. *You have nothing more now than you had the day before you met her.* Aisha may, if *she* chooses, claim you as a father. But that is Aisha's choice, not yours.

THOMAS

You never told me…you disappeared! (He is becoming angry.) and you never told her! *She* had to find me?

GRACE

Yes.

THOMAS

And what lies did you tell her about me?

GRACE

Lies? I told her the truth. I told her that I loved you and that you loved me! (They are staring at each other.) And when I told her that you had died in a car accident…that was not a lie. Because you did die. You died to me that day that you told me you would be going to Rome. It was over that day. Telling her of your "death" was…true in everything except the details.

THOMAS

I looked for you! I prayed that I would find you! I didn't know you were pregnant! I didn't know!

GRACE

You knew that I wasn't going to be a part of your life. You knew you had chosen The Church.

THOMAS

But if I had known! I would have...

GRACE

(Stops him abruptly.)

No. None of your "coulda/shoulda/woulda" nonsense. You decided. You made your choice. And then I made my choice. And if I had only been a better liar, or if Aisha wasn't so curious and so determined to find the truth—or if I had given her a different name—maybe you *still* would not know.

THOMAS

The name was a bit of a give-away.

GRACE

Yeah. But it is such a beautiful name.

THOMAS

Grace...I loved you. And I tried to find you.

GRACE

I know. But that was a long time ago.

(She begins to leave, and he stops her.)

THOMAS

That's it? You drop this...this...bombshell and then you just leave?

GRACE

Yes, that's it. Sometimes the only thing a person can do is just leave. Pick up and go on. You should know that better than anyone.

THOMAS:

OK. I deserved that. But please tell me—is she alright? Is Aisha alright? Is she healthy...?

GRACE

She is healthy. She is in school. She has a part-time job. She seems happy. She doesn't seem to miss her old boyfriend. She is meeting new friends at school.

THOMAS

New friends. Good.

GRACE

What does that mean?

THOMAS

Nothing. I just know so little about her. I guess I am hungry for details.

GRACE

If she wants you to know details, she will contact you. That is her business, not mine. You should know that. (Points to the confessional) Confidentiality is part of *your* business, isn't it?

THOMAS

Yes. Of course. (There is a long pause.) Do you think Aisha will ever come to see me again?

GRACE

That is up to her. She is a big girl. She may decide to see you, or she may not. I will respect her choice—and I expect you to do the same.

THOMAS

But she is so young…

GRACE

She is 18—an adult. And she has me. She has always had me. And she always will.

THOMAS

But…

GRACE

She has a life to live. She has lived it thus far without you, and she—and I—can continue to live our lives without you.

(She assumes the role of a cop, giving an order.)

Do not try to find her. Do not try to contact her. If she chooses to see you, that's up to her. But you will not contact her on your own. Do you understand?

THOMAS

That sounds like an order, Officer. You're pretty good at this cop thing.

GRACE

It is an order. I've been told that lady cops are the worst.

THOMAS

No worse than new, "modern" priests? (She smiles.) Grace?

GRACE

Yes, Thomas?

THOMAS

You know that I loved you, don't you?

GRACE

Yes. And you know that I loved you.

THOMAS

Yes.

GRACE

Well. Enough chit chat. We are both supposed to be working.

 (Points to his collar and to her uniform.)

We are both in uniform today.

 (She then points at the newspaper.)

You look like you have some heavy reading to do.

 (They both smile. GRACE exits SR. THOMAS watches her leave. Curtain.)

End of Play

A Flower for Betty

Andrew Graber

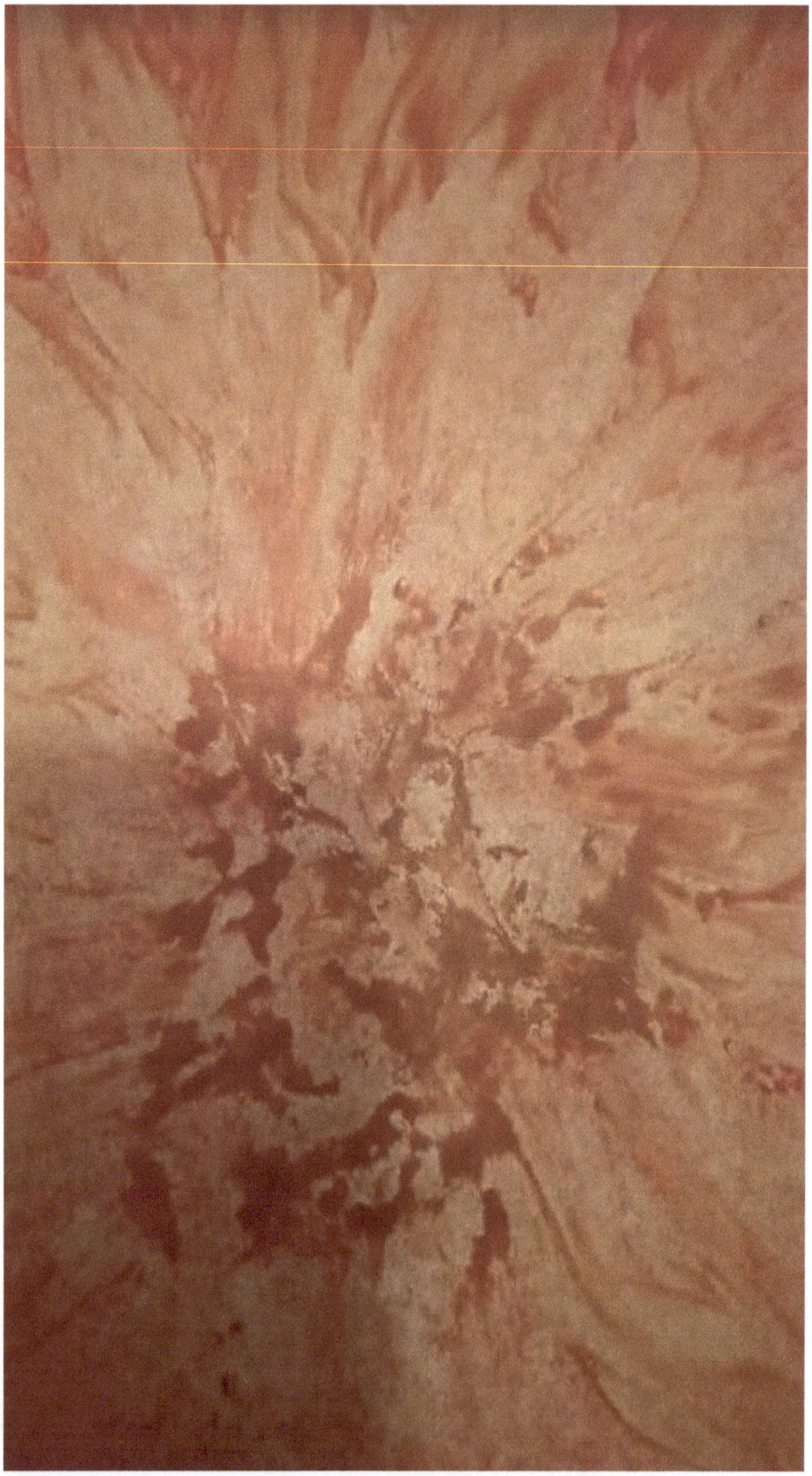

The Good Father

Brian Daldorph

"No, don't be sorry," I say. "Please don't be sorry." I reach over and touch her shoulder. She doesn't flinch at my touch this time.

My daughter's in ER again. She says it was an accident. She took a second dose of pills too soon after the first dose, had a bad reaction to it, called 911.

"Thank God for insurance," she says. "Thank God."

In fact, it wasn't God who signed her up for insurance, it was me, but now's not the time to go into that.

"Thanks for driving here," my daughter says. "I appreciate it."

She's twenty-seven, looks at the same time like she's fifteen and doesn't know a thing about the world and like she's thirty-nine with lines on her face.

"Can you stay here tonight, please?" she says, and I say, "Sure," though I don't know how I'll do it with all the arrangements I'll have to make.

"Thanks," she says. "I know I'll be fine if you're here," and of course I'm thrilled by her faith in me. My marriage is crumbling, I have bills I'll *never* be able to pay off and I've got to call my doctor's office about test results: I know I always say this, but the results will be bad this time.

My daughter's telling me a story about her crazy friend Julie, there's *always* a story about a crazy friend.

I've got so much trouble coming but I do that difficult thing of making the best of good moments while I have them in my hands, before they fall through my fingers and I lose them forever.

Robert

Steve Brisendine

We
linger
over cold
coffees and talk of
our poetry; he has plugged
away at one piece, something with howling roots
in the Beat field, for – here he shrugs, laughs a good-natured
forever. There are no others; he will complete this one, or none at
all—and I, who aim for new words by each midnight, feel myself glib and shallow
in the presence of his devotion. Here is the true poet. Here is the pursuer of words.

Clouds of Memory

Buff Whitman-Bradley

Could it be
That the white puffy clouds
We love to watch
Drifting and shifting
In the amiable atmosphere
Of a warm day in summer
Or a brisk autumn afternoon
Are actually memories
That have escaped,
Or been evicted,
From the cabezas that housed them,
And are now free to wander
The great wide sky
Without any compulsion
To be home and available
For nostalgic conversations
About the good old days,
For disagreements about who
Set Aunt Eugenie's hat on fire
Or who broke Grandfather's crystal snifter?

Will the clouds stay aloft,
And slowly fill with moisture
Which will rain down
Upon the earth?
Will all those memories
Be absorbed by soil,
Swell streams and rivers,
Carry nutrients to forests
And prairie grasses?
Will they slake our thirst
With someone else's amazing journeys,
Someone else's first love?

Illimitable

Michael Moreth

THE TOURNAMENT

One-act play

Ten minutes

Margaret Pearce

SYNOPSIS

A clever wife convinces her husband that running off with his younger secretary is a bad idea.

CHARACTERS

JOHN HENDERSON—VERY trendy middle-aged executive
MARY HENDERSON—middle-aged wife–-plump and comfortable with being middle-aged.
STEVEN HENDERSON—son, late teens
SYLVIA STANTON—secretary, early twenties, glowing with health, confidence and competence.

SCENE 1

Late evening in the Henderson's comfortable lounge room.
Two comfortable chairs each side of fireplace, which is obscured by massed bowl of flowers. Another two seater couch along left wall and door on right wall. The clock on the mantel shows the time at 11 p.m.

MARY HENDERSON relaxed in one of the armchairs watching television and knitting. She is alone. Her feet in their fluffy slippers are up on the footstool. A pile of women's magazines is cascaded on the floor at her feet. A half empty box of chocolates and empty glass of wine on the coffee table in front of her.

Her mobile phone rings. She puts down her knitting, picks up the phone, and turns off the television with the remote control.

MARY
(Placidly)

Hello...yes...this is Mrs. Henderson...Miss Stanton!

(Looks at watch)

Has John had the office working back?...Just dropped you home!...Maringo's? There most nights!...Just talking!

(Incredulous)

MARY, Cont'd

Divorce!...Whose divorce?

(Pulls herself together firmly)

Are you saying that my husband has told you he wants to divorce me?...Made his life hell!

(Starts to grin broadly but keeps her voice grave.)

Begged for his freedom for years!...I <u>quite</u> understand. (Soothingly). Of course, we are all civilized people... . This problem should be talked over...Very sensible of you to ring me ... No- of course it is not too late... (Aside) It is never too late...I shall expect you as soon as you get here. Goodbye, Miss Stanton.

(Closes phone and relaxes back in her chair, selecting another chocolate. She is still grinning.)

MARY

Divorce! Oh John, you wretch.

SCENE 2

The Henderson loungeroom. Clock on mantle showing 11.15 P.M. MARY HENDERSON is knitting, relaxed in her armchair. The door opens. She looks at her watch. JOHN HENDERSON enters.

JOHN

Something wrong with the telly?

MARY

My show finished.

(She is still knitting.)

You're late--working back?

(JOHN strolls across the room and settles in the other armchair. He opens up the paper he was carrying and retires behind it)

JOHN

Had a few things to clear up at the office.

MARY

Working back quite a bit these days aren't you?

JOHN
(Pompous)
The position of executive entails a certain amount of responsibility and a few sacrifices.

                              MARY
Many of the office staff work back with you?

                              JOHN
                           (Yawning)
A few.

                              MARY
Send all the girls home by taxi?

                              JOHN
That's the normal office policy–do you want me to lock up?

                              MARY
Steven can lock up when he gets in.

                              JOHN
Thought the place was quiet. Where is he?

                              MARY
                           (Vague)
He went somewhere with his friends. Your secretary is working very long hours for an
older woman. Did she work back with you tonight?

                              JOHN
                        (Equally vague)
Sylvia's the office dragon–-of course she works back with the usual bunch. Steve still going
out with that smashing blonde?

                              MARY
He headed off with that little dark girl – the quiet one. Did Sylvia go home by taxi?

                              JOHN
That little dark girl has a sweet face–nice if he takes a permanent fancy to her. Actually, I
dropped Sylvia off on my way through tonight.

                              MARY
                           (Sweetly)
The perfect executive, keeping a weather eye on the petty cash.

                              JOHN
              (Up in arms–He gives the paper away as a bad job.).

What is that crack supposed to mean?

                              MARY
                         (Still sweet)
You make a practice of saving on Sylvia's taxi fares. So considerate.

                    JOHN
                  (Dignified)
I often drop staff members off on my way home. (Stands up) I'm going to bed.

                    MARY
                   (Meekly)
I would like to have a few words with you, John. We never ever seem to spend much time
together these days.

                    JOHN
                  (Irritable)
You've had a few words with me–leave it go until the morning.

(Drifts to front of mantel hands in pockets. He sneaks a look at the door which is only three
paces away.)

                    MARY
                   (Humble)
I'm sorry to be so inconsiderate–I realize you have had a tiring night studying...figures.

                    JOHN
                 (Interrupting)
Columns of them–I'm beat.

                    MARY
             (Puts down her knitting)
At Maringo's.

        (There is silence for a few seconds. JOHN tenses. He takes his hand out of his
        pocket to flick at an imaginary piece of lint on his sleeve.)

                    JOHN
                  (Quietly)
Who told you I was at Maringo's tonight?

                    MARY
                  (Casual)
And Monday night and Wednesday night, and every other night you are supposed to be
working back.

                    JOHN
                   (Bored)
So occasionally I grab a bite at Maringo's.... . Is that any reason to start spying on me?

                    MARY
                 (Reproving)
Who said I spied on you.

                              JOHN
              (Working up to righteous indignation)

Cross-examining me the moment I walk in the door. Do I ask you to account for every hour
you put in without supervision?

                              MARY
Sylvia phoned me just before you came in.

                              JOHN
                           (Startled)
Sylvia! What the devil did she want?

                              MARY
                           (Placidly)
She should be here in a few minutes. She was catching a cab around.

                              JOHN
                          (Blustering)
I must say you pick some peculiar hours to entertain your friends.

                              MARY

<u>Your</u> friend, John

                              JOHN
                          (Hopefully)
She had some work she was finishing–but it wasn't necessary for her to make a special trip
                   for it. That woman is just too conscientious.

                              MARY
                           (Echoing)
<u>Much</u> too conscientious.

                              JOHN
You should have told her to leave it until Monday.

                              MARY
                           (Emphasis)
<u>This</u> matter isn't waiting until Monday, and she is not bringing any work around.

                              JOHN
                           (Worried)
So why is she coming?

                              MARY
Why do you think?

JOHN
(Blustering again)
I think you're turning neurotic. It's a pity you can't find anything better to do than cross-examine me every time I put a foot inside the door.

(The door bell rings. MARY gets up and goes out of the room.)

JOHN
(Finishing his speech to her departing back)
You don't expect me to entertain your guest this hour of the night do you? I'm going to bed–give my apologies to Miss Stanton when she gets here.

(He moves toward the door. It opens. MARY ushers in SYLVIA STANTON. JOHN retreats back to his armchair and sits with his head in his hands for a split second.)

Mary
(Gracious)
Do come in Miss Stanton. I'm Mary Henderson. So glad you could come.

SYLVIA
(Brightly)
Hi, Mrs. Henderson–you don't look a bit like what I imagined you would.

MARY
(Drily)
Neither do you.

(JOHN stands for a few seconds and then sits down again.)

JOHN
(Awkward)
Evening, Sylvia.

SYLVIA
(Direct)
Are you surprised to see me here, John?

(SYLVIA crosses over and sits on the edge of the two seater couch. MARY picks up her knitting.)

JOHN
Why yes.

SYLVIA
(Reasonable)
Surely after our conversation the reason is obvious.

                              JOHN
                           (Imploring)
Sylvia.

                              MARY
                          (Reassuring)
No need to be shy John. Miss Stanton and I feel it is time we discussed this problem of
yours openly.

                             SYLVIA
                            (Nicely)
Just call me Sylvia. Everyone else does.

                              JOHN
           (Even more desperate at his wife's reassuring tone)

What problem?

                              MARY
            (The reassurance has gone, and she is ironic.)
What problem indeed! What about my continual refusal to dissolve our loveless marriage
because of my social position?

                              JOHN
                    (Embarrassed and humble)
Now Mary.

                             SYLVIA
                        (Matter of factly)
You don't look at all like a society matron type.

                              MARY
               (Continuing in pretend surprise)
No problem! When you have been tied for years to someone who has made your life hell
with their irrational jealousy and hysterical scenes!

                             SYLVIA
                           (Eagerly)
Johnnie! I know you are too softhearted to hurt a fly, but you have been taken advantage of
for years. Be firm. Mrs. Henderson and I have discussed the whole thing in a civilized
manner over the phone. She agrees that she wouldn't hold you to a loveless marriage and
will be happy to proceed with a divorce.

                              JOHN

               (He is so shocked he stands.)
Oh! My God–Mary!

MARY
(Calmly)
Sit down John. As Sylvia said, we're civilized people. (Touch of sarcasm) If only I had
known how unhappy you were I would have put you out of your misery years ago.

SYLVIA
(Gently)
He's been trying to break it to you for months, but he didn't want to upset you.

MARY

How many months?

        (SYLVIA stands and starts to pace around the room restlessly. SYLVIA is and always
        has been a creature of action.)

SYLVIA
A lifetime! A full four months (Defiantly) I'm glad it's out in the open. I haven't liked all
this pretense. (Proudly) I want Johnnie at my side—as the man I love, not as someone to be
ashamed of, terrified of being seen together, always dodging people we know.

        (The silence lengthens. SYLVIA sits down again and waits expectantly.)

JOHN
(Uncertain)
These things happen Mary and get out of control.

MARY
(Tart)

I can see the lack of control.

JOHN
(Authoritative)
Look! We're all tired. We can discuss this at some more appropriate time. I'm going to bed.

        (JOHN rises from his chair.)

MARY
(All polite interest)

Whose bed?

        (SYLVIA walks back and sits down, hands on chin and watches JOHN expectantly.)

SYLVIA

Yes Johnnie. That is a good question.

JOHN
(Voice rising as he starts pacing)
Damn you, Mary. This entire mess is your fault. Making my life hell with your prying
questions—always needling me. Always out with your Women's Auxiliaries. The whole

JOHN, Cont'd

thing wouldn't have happened if you had put yourself out to come out with me occasionally and socialized occasionally with my business associates.

MARY

You always objected to overlapping your business and social life before.

JOHN
(Continuing a long list of grievances)

And it's damn nice to take out someone who is interested in my golf handicap, and can take an intelligent interest in the cricket scores and be bothered dressing up to go out.

(The door opens. STEVEN strolls into the room, nearly colliding with his father.)

STEVEN

Gee Dad. What are you yelling about? You can be heard all over the neighbourhood. (Notices SYLVIA.) Hi Sylvie. What are you doing here?

JOHN
(Stiff)

You know Miss Stanton, my secretary?

(STEVEN strolls across to sit beside SYLVIA.)

STEVEN

Of course. Sylvia played in the mixed doubles with me last week.

(JOHN walks back to his chair and collapses back into it.)

JOHN
(Trying for the casual approach)

We're just having a quiet discussion. Isn't it past your bed time?

STEVEN

Didn't sound very quiet.

MARY
(Amused)

As this is a family discussion you may as well stay. Your father wants to marry Sylvia.

STEVEN
(Horrified and disbelieving)

Grow up, Dad. Nice sort of fool I would look at the tennis club if my old Dad ran off with our best player.

JOHN
(Fuming)

You impertinent…. Keep a civil tongue in your head.

MARY
(Reproving from habit)

Don't be rude to your father, Steven.

SYLVIA

Well thank you, Steve. We are still on top then? I didn't stay long enough after that last game to find out.

STEVEN

Right on top of the ladder–a real dizzy position, and I'm fast getting a head for heights.

JOHN
(Sullen and backing to the protection of the mantel)

The fact is, Steven. For some reason your mother seems determined to push me into this position–heaven knows why!

(SYLVIA stands up and walks over and puts her hand on JOHN's arm.)

SYLVIA
(Slowly)

Johnnie you said tonight that material things don't mean a thing–that the basic things in life were the most important–that we belonged together.

JOHN
(Embarrassed)

Well, that is true in a manner of speaking.

(SYLVIA removes her hand from his arm.)

SYLVIA
(Coldly)

In a manner of speaking?

JOHN
(Wretched)

There is no need to get the entire matter out of proportion.

STEVEN

Going to look a bit silly without some of those unimportant material things, aren't you, Dad?

JOHN

What do you mean?

                                STEVEN
          (He is enjoying being nasty.)

Who gets the house, the car, half a share of the business and all your superannuation to
console her? Getting a bit slow in your old age aren't you.

                                 JOHN
                             (Disbelieving)
Why you....

                                STEVEN
Do you think Mum is going to walk out of her home and garden to make room for Sylvia?
And what am I supposed to do—which parent do I take custody of or do we all live together
like one big happy family? Will you put Mum in the spare room and keep her for a
houseguest?

                                SYLVIA
                              (Accusing)
You told me your wife had been installed in the spare room since Steve was a baby!

                                 MARY
                              (Amused)
Only when he gets a bad attack of his gout. He can't even bear to have anyone moving
around in the same room.

                                SYLVIA
                              (Blankly)
Gout!

                                 JOHN
                              (Goaded)
Really, Mary! Is this conversation necessary?

                                 MARY
                               (Firm)
Most necessary. Sylvia should know how to nurse you with your gout. (To SYLVIA) I'll give
you his prescription. He never remembers to collect it in time, and he is crippled if he
doesn't start them early enough.

                                SYLVIA
Cripppled! Johnnie! You love me and I love you. It is as simple as that–pack your things
and come back to the flat with me.

                                 JOHN
                             (Embarrassed)
It's never that uncomplicated, Sylvia.

MARY
(Is she trying to be helpful?)
And don't forget your gold clubs. The big tournament is tomorrow.

JOHN
Good heavens! My golf tournament! I had completely forgotten   - I wanted to approach old
Poples about the merger – I must work on those figures tonight.

SYLVIA
(Drily)
If your golf match is more important than us?

JOHN
(Stands and starts to pace up and down)
The merger is important–you know that. It means my bread and butter for the next twelve
months.

SYLVIA
(Sarcastic)
What about rather living on bread and water with me than steak and champagne without
me?

JOHN
(Abstracted)
Yes of course, Sylvia. That's very true. (To himself) I can't seem too obvious in my
approach–I'll jot the figures on the back of a score card. (Absently) Mary, is that shirt with
the zip pocket clean?

MARY
Yes, and I had your golf shoes resoled. (To syliva politely) Perhaps he can join you
tomorrow night, Miss Stanton.

JOHN
(Detached)
Yes, perhaps tomorrow night, Sylvia.

(SYLVIA stands up and shakes herself.)

SYLVIA
(Polite)
No thank you, Mr. Henderson. I think I'll be busy tomorrow night. (Puts out hand to
MARY) Goodbye, Mrs. Henderson, so <u>educational</u> meeting you. (Walks over and pulls
STEVEN to his feet.) Come on, Steve, drive me home.

STEVE
(Takes SYLVIA's arm and heads towards the door.)
No probs. Back in twenty minutes, Mum. Leave some coffee for me, will you?

(They exit.)

(There is silence for a few seconds. JOHN starts fidgeting. MARY puts her knitting away carefully.)

MARY
(There is nothing in her voice)
You will have a big day tomorrow–you had better get to bed. I'll bring your coffee in. Work on your figures in the morning. Your mind will be a lot clearer.

JOHN
(Hesitant)
Mary! There appears to be a few things I should like to explain.

MARY
This evening has been very self-explanatory. Do you want me to set the alarm early?

JOHN
Yes thanks. Make it for 6 a.m. (Pause) About Sylvia…

MARY
She seems a sensible and intelligent young woman (Pause) to run your office. (Amused) You want to think seriously about the choices between bread and butter and steak and champagne lifestyles. Do you want milk coffee?

JOHN
(Even meeker at this reminder)
Yes please, and I'll have some of those shortbread biscuits to go with it. About that other business, I never really meant…

MARY
I know.

(She is so dry that JOHN flinches. She relents.)

Go to bed John. I'll put the coffee on.

OoooOoooo

Snowy Meadow

Karen Colstrom

Basket-Weavers of Santa Fe

John Grey

Basket-weavers hunch close together
by the crumbling walls
of the long abandoned fort.
Steady fingers guide strands of yucca
in and out of each other,
plait their wefts and warps,
pull them tight as gritted teeth.
The sun is searing.
The shadows barely stretch to their knees.
But if they don't do this,
only ghosts will.

Moonrise

Patricia L. Hamilton

"Tropical" summoned picture-book toucans,
"sultry" a word I'd only read.
But this air was alive—leaf-riffling eddies,
frond-flashing currents swirling
through bougainvillea-bright pinks and reds,
the warm sea-scent sweeping our taxi
through a vibrant cityscape stitched with tourist-trade
to our hotel, sentried by purple-orange Birds of Paradise,
afternoon clouds mounding in white masses on the horizon.

I'd encountered aquamarine—
my birthstone, the pool I swam in each summer.
But this water astonished, an exuberance of blues,
pale shallows striated into pellucid azure,
wisp-shadows dappling the sparkling sheen,
beach-bathers beading the white sand-necklace
as transistors blared over children's squeals,
in the distance the rumpled brown pleat-folds
of Diamond Head ascending to their iconic peak.

Dixieland was familiar
from summer band concerts in the park.
But this jazz burned a hole in the night,
the combo in the courtyard bar conversing
at a lazy island tempo, smart-alecky trumpet
trading barbs with a growling trombone,
both sweet-talking the clarinet, whose sassy replies
were sinuous as the breeze, the sound of surf breaking
on the beach as steady as the drummer's brushwork.

I'd gazed at the moon
hanging above the mountains that flanked my hometown.
But this moon seared itself into my memory:
a perfect, luminous orb ascending serenely
behind silhouetted coconut palms and glittering hotels,
the fresh ocean air ruffling my hair as I sat on the balcony,
reluctantly left behind by aunties off to see Don Ho,
reveling in my solitude, entranced by the night-music—
a gift as exotic and intoxicating as a sip from a magic potion.

Random Act of Kindness

Patricia L. Hamilton

September 9, 2001

You scoured the Internet for a fancy restaurant
open on Sunday, looking to splurge

for our sixth anniversary: our lean years
in grad school at last yielding

a new refrigerator, washer, and dryer
in our new condo, never mind

my loneliness in a new city, or the grind
of your weekly commute, 400 miles each way.

We agreed on Japanese, only to find ourselves
seated at a u-shaped *teppanyaki* table

with a dozen strangers, watching a daredevil
juggling his Ginsu knives, not our idea

of a romantic dinner for two.
Too polite to withdraw, we traded

furtive smiles and held hands under the table,
the steak and *o-sushi* rice plentiful.

A gray-haired man in a golf shirt
kept the college girls down the table laughing.

Grandfather? Or natural-born comedian?
When you slid out your wallet,

the chef waved you off, nodding
toward the older man's retreating back.

"He paid for everyone. Whole table.
The world holds some good men, *ne*?"

Variegated Fritillary on Butterfly Weed

Karen Colstrom

HUNGER PAINS

A Screenplay

Mark Blickley

Synopsis:

    Hunger Pains is a short, dark comedic film chronicling a Baby Boomer romance circa 2023 that is fueled by the social media dating app, Bumble. It takes food porn to dizzying new heights as ANCA, a highly eccentric Romanian-born alpha female who is fiercely self-sufficient and lives her life according to her own rules and views and doesn't give a damn about what others think of her behavior and lifestyle, invites ARNOLDO (after selecting him from the Bumble app) to her home for a first date homecooked meal that is much more animal autopsy than culinary treat. Arnoldo is a genuinely nice guy who is desperately horny. The entire meal is an intense balancing act for him not to alienate Anca's possible affection that could be turned into the sexual favors he so intensely desires.

FADE IN:

INSERT TITLE: *BUMBLE STUMBLE*

INT—CLOSE UP as a finger swipes at a smartphone app. We hear 2:39-2:48 from "Blessing of Nature." https://www.youtube.com/watch?v=oecQDr9B6KU

We see ANCA'S hand holding her smartphone that's open at the dating app BUMBLE. She quickly swipes her finger past a few profiles until she lands on the Bumble page of ARNOLDO LEGASPI. At the bottom of a photo of two smiling men it reads:

ARNOLDO, 57
Blood of the Virgin Community College

ANCA places her finger on ONUR's face.

ANCA (O.S.)

    Ah, my Bumble caveman!

EXT—HOUSE ENTRANCE

ARNOLDO LEGASPI walks up the pathway to ANCA'S house. We cannot see his face, but he is carrying a guitar case and a bouquet of flowers. He walks up the steps and presses the doorbell button.

INT—HOUSE

We hear the doorbell ring.

INSERT TITLE: *GENTLEMAN CALLER*

ANCA appears and walks towards the door holding a large horsehead mask. We see her from behind. She is wearing a silk robe with a dragon stitched on its back. ANCA pauses by the staircase banister and puts the horse mask on its knob before opening the door.

EXT–HOUSE ENTRANCE

We see ARNOLDO looking up at ANCA. His face wreaths into a wide-eyed look of surprise and lusty excitement.

                    ARNOLDO
(gasps)
          Hello. I....I'm Arnoldo Legaspi. You must be Anca?

ARNOLDO hands ANCA the flowers.

ANCA looks down at him and then past him, leaning her head out the doorway looking to his left and right, searching. Beneath her open robe she is wearing sexy lingerie.

                    ANCA
          Yes. I am she. Who was the other man in your Bumble profile photo?

ANCA grabs his flowers.

                    ARNOLDO
          That's my good friend, Rhinehardt.

                    ANCA
          Why do so many men not pose by themselves in their Bumble profiles?

                    ARNOLDO
          I can't speak for others, but I use that picture of Rhinehardt and me because
          when I just use my own photo I don't get half the hits. And as you know, on
          Bumble the woman must initiate contact.

                    ANCA
(clears throat)
          You are an honest man. Good.

(ANCA sniffs flowers.)

          These have no smell.

                    ARNOLDO
          Sorry.

ANCA
When one is decapitated, it should always smell like fear.

CUT TO:

ARNOLDO
That makes sense.

ANCA tosses the flowers onto her lawn, balls the paper up in her fist. She looks ARNOLDO up and down in a penetrating inspection.

ANCA
Come in.

INT—House Vestibule

ANCA tosses bouquet paper into vestibule trashcan and walks ahead to the kitchen. We see ARNOLDO following her, licking his chops in joyful erotic anticipation. He pauses to look at the strange horse head mask on the banister.

ANCA (points)
You may place your guitar in the living room.

INT—KITCHEN

ANCA leads ARNOLDO to his seat at her kitchen table where there are two place settings and a small basket of bread. They are both seated.

ARNOLDO (smiles)
I was very surprised to get your dinner invitation for a first date. Usually women insist on grabbing a cup of coffee somewhere in a public space.

ANCA
I hate caffeine. Coffee just makes people more nervous, gives them the shits and causes breast tissue cysts.

ARNOLDO (nods)
I hear you.

ANCA (fondles her breasts)
These babies are as smooth as a baboon's ass.

ARNOLDO
Are they?

ANCA
Or the top of your head. May I touch your skull?

                              ARNOLDO
Please.
He bends his head towards her.

                               ANCA
Do not bow! Keep your head erect!

                              ARNOLDO
Sorry, Anca.

                               ANCA
ANCA rubs both hands over his head.

        Ah, very smooth no lumps but here, some strong bumps that indicate virtue
        and virility. Hmmm….and low esteem.

                              ARNOLDO
Really?

                               ANCA
Yes. I am a student of phrenology.

                              ARNOLDO
It feels wonderful. Is that some kind of massage therapy?

                   ANCA (withdraws her hands)
What? Phrenology is the science that shows how the shape of your head
determines the shape of your mind and character.

                              ARNOLDO
I was never good in science.

                               ANCA
I'm sure you know enough to keep yourself hydrated. Would you like a
beverage?

                              ARNOLDO
Yes.

                               ANCA
Do you enjoy herbal tea?

                              ARNOLDO
I enjoy herb tea and anything organic.

                               ANCA
Organic! You fall for that vicious labeling?

                    ARNOLDO (stuttering)
Well....uh....it's......

                         ANCA
They label processed food organic, when it is no longer a product of the
earth!

                        ARNOLDO
The bastards!

                         ANCA
What herb tea do you prefer?

                        ARNOLDO
I....er....like....enjoy green tea. Do you have any?

                         ANCA
Absolutely not. It contains caffeine.

                        ARNOLDO
Oh my god, I feel so...used.

                         ANCA
I drink Chinese white tea made from Narcissus and chai cha bushes.

                        ARNOLDO
That sounds challenging---like a stuck up dancer.

                         ANCA
What do you mean?

                        ARNOLDO
I don't know. I heard narcissus and chai cha bushes and I thought of the cha-
cha...

                         ANCA
You were being humorous?

                        ARNOLDO
Apparently not.

                         ANCA
Do you dance?

                        ARNOLDO
A little. But I prefer to help people dance by playing my guitar.

                    ANCA
Good. Very good. I love to dance. Perhaps after dinner your fingers can guide
me into a rollicking romp.

ANCA retrieves tea pot from stove.

                    ARNOLDO
I look forward to it.

ANCA pours tea into his cup.

                    ANCA
White tea.

                    ARNOLDO
It looks delicious. (He sniffs it, scrunches his face)

                    ANCA
It's very good for the bowels, Arnoldo.

                    ARNOLDO
Thank you, Anca.

ARNOLDO takes a sip, grimaces and spits it back into the cup.

                    ANCA
It displeases you?

                    ARNOLDO
No, no. I love it. Sipping it just makes me think of white privilege.

                    ANCA
You're a very sensitive person, Arnoldo.

                    ARNOLDO
You're not kidding. I break out in rashes all the time. Nothing contagious.

                    ANCA
Are you being funny?

                    ARNOLDO
That's not for me to say.

                    ANCA
Good answer. Please tell me a joke.

                    ARNOLDO
Here's one I heard at work. Have you ever heard of Virginia Pip-a-lean-nee?

                    ANCA (shakes head)
Who?

                    ARNOLDO
Virginia Pip-a-lean-nee. Are you Catholic?

                    ANCA
No.

                    ARNOLDO
Good. Three nuns were driving through the Lincoln Tunnel where they had a
head-on collision. All three died and their souls rose to heaven. They were
met at heaven's gate by St. Peter. He told them he had reviewed their files
and, since all had led such exemplary lives of piety and faith, the Lord
decreed they could return to earth and become whomever they'd like. So, St.
Peter asks the first nun who she would like to return as and she says, "Oh St.
Peter, I'd love to return as Beyonce." St. Peters nods, "okay" and writes it in
his book. He asks the second nun who she would like to be and she says, "Oh
Please, St. Peter, return me as Lady Gaga." "Done," and he writes it in the
book. Then he turns to the third nun, the Mother Superior and most devout
of the three and asks her. She says, "could you please return me as Virginia
Pip-a-lean-i?" St. Peter is about to write the name in the book and pauses.
"Virginia Pipeline?" I'd love to honor your request, Sister, but I don't know
who Virginia Pipeline is?" Mother Superior reaches inside her habit and pulls
out a yellow, crumpled newspaper clipping. "Perhaps this can help you? She
holds up the article and the headline reads, "400 Men Lay Virginia Pipeline
in 3 days."

                    ANCA
I don't get it.

                    ARNOLDO
I guess you have to be Catholic.

                    ANCA
Are you hungry?

                    ARNOLDO
Famished.

                    ANCA
I made soup as an appetizer. Do you like soup?

                    ARNOLDO (smiles)
Of course. Especially if it's homemade.

INSERT TITLE: *First Course*

ANCA goes to stove and dishes out two bowls of soup. Each bowl has a large bone inside. She places a bowl at her seat and gives one to ARNOLDO.

                    ARNOLDO (looks horrified)
          It looks...um tasty. (picks up bone) What kind of meat is this?
                              ANCA
          It's a Bovine femur.

                    ARNOLDO (under his breath)
          This isn't a meal, it's an autopsy.

                              ANCA
          Did you say something, Arnoldo?

                    ARNOLDO (shakes head)
          No. No.

                              ANCA
          It's the thigh and strongest bone in the body. I love sucking on the strongest
          bone in the body and swallowing its protein rich marrow.

ARNOLDO dips his spoon into the soup but can't take his eyes off ANCA's lusty, sucking of the femur. The camera cuts back and forth between her determined, erotic sucking of the bone and his enthralled, heightened sexual arousal watching her. At one point, we see ARNOLDO with sweat dripping down his face that he quickly wipes away with his sleeve.

                    ANCA (completes marrow sucking)
          Oh my god!

                              ARNOLDO
          Oh my god!

They each spew out, 'Oh my god," as if echoing a joint orgasm. ANCA looks at his bowl and sees his bone untouched.

                              ANCA
          Arnoldo, you haven't touched your bone. Do you mind if I suck on it?

                    ARNOLDO (hands it to her)
          Are you kidding? Here...take it. Take it.

                    ANCA (smiles)
          Thank you.

We hear slurping sounds as the camera shows ARNOLDO in a state of voyeuristic ecstasy.

CLOSE UP---ANCA'S MOUTH SUCKING ON BONE MARROW

CUT TO:

We will spritz ARNOLDO's head, so it looks like he's broken out in a sweat watching her as we hear her slurping sounds.

INSERT TITLE: *SECOND COURSE*

> ANCA
>
> Do you like chicken?

> ARNOLDO
>
> Yes.

> ANCA
>
> Do you prefer the ass or the feet?

> ARNOLDO (dismayed)
>
> Ah.....um.....feet. Feet.

> ANCA
>
> Good. As do I.

ANCA retrieves a bowl of chicken feet.

CLOSE UP: Bowl of chicken feet.

She dishes some on ARNOLDO's plate and then on her own plate. He looks bewildered at all those tiny feet and then up at ANCA.

CUT TO: Close up of ANCA with five chicken feet sticking out of her mouth. When she speaks it looks as if the chicken is dancing within her mouth.

> ANCA
>
> You aren't eating. Do they displease you?

> ARNOLDO
>
> I was just....you know, wondering what you meant by chicken ass.

> ANCA
>
> My English isn't descriptive?

> ARNOLDO
>
> Being descriptive is not a problem you have, Anca.

> ANCA
>
> The ass. The chicken's fleshy backside

> ARNOLDO
>
> I see. In Latin it's called the cloaca.

                              ANCA
        Exactly.

CUT TO:
ARNOLDO spits out a chicken's foot.

                              ANCA
        Arnoldo, are you nervous?

                              ARNOLDO
        I'm almost relaxing.

INSERT TITLE: *THIRD COURSE*

                              ANCA
        I don't usually make this offer to men I don't know, but I was impressed with
        your friend's photo.

                              ARNOLDO
        He'll be happy to hear it. I'll certainly tell him. What is your offer?

                              ANCA
        I would like to give you some head.

ARNOLDO does a double take and is speechless.

                              ANCA
        Do you have any objections to me giving you head?

                        ARNOLDO (shakes head)
        No. None. Zero. Nada.

                        ANCA (seductively)
        Then I suggest you loosen your belt and wait for me in the dining room. I'll be
        right with you.

                        ARNOLDO (beaming)
        Thank you, Anca.

She leaves; ARNOLDO does a jig for joy as he rises, walks into the dining room and loosens
his belt.

CUT TO:
ANCA walks into the dining room carrying a plate with a cooked lamb's head, complete
with eyeballs.

                              ANCA
        What are you doing? Why are you standing there with your pants down!?

ARNOLDO (embarrassed)
I was loosening my belt as you suggested, and my pants accidently slipped. *(He pulls up his pants.)* Sorry.

ANCA
I told you to loosen your belt because this is such a big, meaty head I thought you'd get stuffed since you've barely eaten anything else.

ARNOLDO (points to head)
But it's staring at me!

ANCA
Hmmmm... Then tell me what the lamb sees.

She places the head on the table.

ARNOLDO
It sees a grateful man appreciative of a woman who would go to such great lengths to make him feel comfortable.

ANCA
Are you being truthful?

ARNOLDO
Am I being truthful? I live by the motto," there comes a time in the affairs of every man when they must grab the bull by the tail, and face the situation."

ANCA
Ahhhhhhhh.....I love ox tails.

ARNOLDO
That's a surprise.

ANCA removes a hatchet from the cabinet.

ANCA (points to head)
So there it is. Something else must die in our place. There are very few things in this world you can eat that doesn't require a death.

ARNOLDO
Not to get biblical, but what about milk and honey?

ANCA
Ah, you work at Blood of the Virgin Community College. Milk and honey are excretions.

ARNOLDO
But its enzymes are considered living.

ANCA (smiles)
True. The different flavored energies we swallow from the creatures we eat
are the stored sunlight we need in order to survive.

When Arnoldo sees Anca smile, he's determined to continue to impress her.

ARNOLDO
May I say a prayer over the head of this sacrificial lamb?

ANCA
If you must.

ARNOLDO (bows head)
Heavenly Father to you I pray,
A majestic creature may come my way.
Let my aim be straight and true.
This my Lord I pray to you.
Take his spirit swift and fast.
For his last breath should not be,
one of pain and agony.
Let his soul come to thee.
To roam your heavens,
wild and free.

ANCA
That is such bullshit! Humans don't have souls and neither do animals.

ARNOLDO
Ah, you were brought up Communist. Anca, St. Anthony is the patron saint of
butchers.

ANCA (angry)
What do you know of butchering and butchers?

ARNOLDO
I know our neighborhood butcher, Stevie Katz, had an affair with my mother
that led to her divorcing my father.

ANCA
Of course your mother would be attracted to a butcher! Have you ever killed
anything you've eaten?

ARNOLDO
No, except for the marriage to my ex-wife.

ANCA
I don't put anything into my mouth that I haven't killed, plucked, or fucked!

                              ARNOLDO
          You killed this lamb?

                                ANCA
          Of course! I travel many hours Upstate to a free-range farm and select the
          animals I will destroy and consume.

                              ARNOLDO
          Ah, so you can thank them in person for giving their lives for you.

                                ANCA
          These animals aren't giving me their lives for my dinner. I'm taking it. If you
          steal someone's car, do you thank her for the gift?

                              ARNOLDO
          Depends on whether she left me a full tank or not.

                                ANCA
          Well, there's plenty of this baby to fill up on. Do you mind if I eat the left eye?
          I'm superstitious.

                         ARNOLDO (repulsed)
          Not at all. Be my guest.

ANCA plucks out the left eye and pops it into her mouth.

                                ANCA
          Arnoldo, do you know what the tastiest part of the head is?

                       ARNOLDO (shakes head)
          No. I'm straight.

                                ANCA
          The brains!

ANCA slams the hatchet into the skull.

CUT TO:

ARNOLDO has brain matter splattered onto the top of his head. ANCA goes to him with
paper towels and gently wipes it up. He moves his head with each of her strokes as if he's a
cat receiving loving strokes. She then inhales the dirty paper towel as if it is a fragrance.

INSERT TITLE: *FOURTH COURSE*

ANCA and ARNOLDO are seated back at the kitchen table.

                                    ANCA
You didn't eat any head or bone marrow soup or chicken feet. You must be
hungry.

                                  ARNOLDO
I have more of a passion than a hunger.

                                    ANCA
Hmmmmm..... Do you like coconut.

                            ARNOLDO (excitedly)
I love coconut!

                                    ANCA
Good. That's dessert.

She retrieves a coconut and places it in his hand.

                                    ANCA
        Shake it.

                                  ARNOLDO
                (stands, shakes coconut and his booty)
        Sounds juicy!

ANCA snatches the coconut and smashes it open on the floor with her hatchet.

CUT TO:
ARNOLDO winces as if he's being castrated.

INSERT TITLE: *SERENADE*

                        ANCA (in hallway by banister)
        I'm going to change into something more appropriate for our musical soiree.

ANCA points to the living room as we see her walking up the steps, passing the horse head.

ARNOLDO goes to couch and warms up his instrument.

CUT TO:

ANCA descends the steps in her red dress. Arnoldo stops his tuning. She walks over to him.

                                  ARNOLDO
Oh my God! You look so hot you could be arrested for global warming.

                                    ANCA
Have you ever been arrested?

                              ARNOLDO
Not yet. Have you?

                               ANCA
Just once in this country.

                              ARNOLDO
For what?
                               ANCA
I was arrested for peeing on my ex-lover's grave at Green-Wood Cemetery.

                              ARNOLDO
Wow, you must've been really angry at him.

                               ANCA
Absolutely not! I adored the man.

                              ARNOLDO
So why did you pee on his grave?

                               ANCA
I was just crying from the place I miss him most.

CUT TO:
Close Up on ARNOLDO furrowing his eyebrows.

                               ANCA
So what are you going to play for me?

                              ARNOLDO
What would you like me to play?

                               ANCA
Why do you ask me that? I am a dancer! You are the man and must take the
lead.

                              ARNOLDO
Sure. No problem. I'm fond of improv although I always name my guitar riffs.
In honor of your wonderful meal tonight I'm going to call this composition,
"The Dance of a Thousand Tongues."

                            ANCA (smiles)
Ah! Sounds delicious!

ARNOLDO begins to play his guitar as ANCA follows his lead. He begins slow but builds up
momentum until by the end of the tune where he thrashes the notes and ANCA collapses in
an orgasmic-like frenzy on the couch, smiling up at him.

INSERT TITE: *SOCIAL INTERCOURSE*

We see ANCA sashaying up the stairs. She turns her head and looks down at the steps

CUT TO:
An over the shoulder shot of her looking down at ARNOLDO, crouched on all fours following her up the steps while wearing the horse's head. When he appears on screen, we hear O:11 –the horse's cry from "Blessings of Nature."

FADE TO BLACK as we hear continuation of "Blessings of Nature" as the credits role.

I Forgot There Were Stars

Suzanna C. de Baca

I forgot there were stars
because I was looking straight ahead.
Shining street lamps, glaring headlights
the noise of traffic and sirens,
the smell of exhaust.

I forgot there were stars
because I was looking to the left and the right
head down, focused on facts,
screens blinking, paper in my hands,
breaking news like rushing water;
in meetings, in the grocery store
pumping gas, loading laundry
scurrying like an ant, urgently moving
crumbs, spinning in circles.

But then one cold winter night I saw them:
so dark, so quiet as I walked along the path.
The screech of an owl pierced me and I fell
headlong into the blackness of the midnight sky.

The constellations held me. For a split second
my life unfolded. Moments I had shoved down
so deep I could not feel them any more
came rushing up, all the loss, longing, doubt
and joys I had dismissed: the mystery
of an eclipse, a hawk slowly gliding
against the cloud, the silence after
a snowfall, freshly cut hayfields.

I inhaled and exhaled, and was overcome
with stillness. Then the heavens
threw me back and whispered, *Look up.*

Saturn's Rings Are Disappearing

Suzanna C. de Baca

Seven rings of ice and dust in the sky,
luminous, flaming hula hoops spinning
like dervishes. The brightest of them all,
a beacon, pulsating, whirring. I can see you
now with my naked eye. But your light
is disappearing.

Your rings were the last to be formed.
Gravitational instability exploded
and frozen moons burst into fragments,
glowing circles, swirling crowns
trumpeting your presence.

Oh, the other planets' rings were young
once too, all energy and speed, radiant
in the opaque landscape of space. Now,
they are dimming with time, moving
more slowly, so faint in the distance.

I thought we would grow old together,
fade gracefully, but you are losing mass,
getting weaker. Like Saturn's rings,
you beamed. You blazed. You kicked up
soil and snow, traversed the earth,
a spoke in motion, vibrant and joyous,
your essence illuminating those
around you. But you are leaving us.
There is so little time now.

The brilliance of earlier light fades
but is no less beautiful as it dissipates.
Each ring has its fleeting moment
and is gone. We are just travelers
passing through the sea of infinity,
whirling wheels, halos in the sky.

Hurricane Kay Clouds Approach

Gerald Uyeno

CORPORAL MARGARET HASTINGS, 1914-1978

Monologue

Judith Present

SYNOPSIS
A woman who survived a plane crash during World War II tells her story.

I was always a little different. When my girlfriends were getting married and eager to have children, I was dreaming of something else. I was dreaming of adventure and okay I was a little boy crazy, but I liked men and knowing how to attract them was always fun. But I didn't necessarily find the marrying kind attractive; I liked the ones who had adventure pasted on their foreheads.

I came from upstate New York in the little town of Owego by the Susquehanna River. My mother worked at a factory that made boots for the Army. My father had died, and she had to work to support us, but to me she looked like she was trudging to work in the same boots she helped make. As I watched her, I knew that wouldn't be me. And I daydreamed about what I could do to see the world. And when a chance came to me, I took it.

The only women who could join the US Army were nurses, but by 1944 there were openings for women to join the men, under the Women's Army Corps, and I joined 150,000 women from around the country as WACS. (salutes)

When they told me I would be going to a little island off of Australia called New Guinea I was ecstatic, jumping up and down. I, little Margaret Hastings, was off to the see the world. But, of course, at that time I had no idea the world I would be seeing. At that time, some would say I was out of control with my new found freedom and the love of men soon made me something attuned to a show girl.

By May 1945 right before the end of the war with Japan a gang of us from the base got into an Air Force C-47 Skytrain, The Gremlin Special to see some sites around the island. There were 24 of us who set out with the pilots telling us about strange tribes on the island, where naked men of super powers lived, and we were all so excited and laughing. When I look back now, we all seemed so silly and unconscious of what could happen. But in showing off, our plane's pilot flew to low and hit a mountainside. And it hit hard; all of us were thrown out of our seats.

At first, I was stunned and mad that this could stop us from seeing the natives they told us about. Then I wasn't' sure where I was, was I home, was I in my bed, was this a dream, but my first realization was I was lying on a dead person who had their arms around me, and the plane was in flames with the smell of gasoline. I began now to think clearly and crawled to the nearest exit.

148

When I got out, I saw there were a few others still alive, some in very critical condition. I was burned, my face was throbbing in pain, and I had no shoes on. As I finally looked around and realized what our predicament was, I was really frightened. We were in the densest jungle, and we hardly had any food, just some candy. We had finally seen our dilemma.

Laura Besley and Eleanor Hanna, two of my best friends, were lying next to each other on the ground where Lt. McCollom had placed them, after getting them out of the plane. I knelt by Eleanor. She didn't seem to be in pain, but I could see it was already too late to do anything for her. The fire had burnt off all her clothes, leaving Eleanor with unbelievable burns all over her entire body. Only her angelic, pink-cheeked face was unscarred. And I could tell she knew what I knew. She looked at me with pleading eyes and gave me a feeble smile. "Let's sing," she said, and we tried but it didn't happen. I looked over to Laura and she was already gone. After a hard cry I took Laura shoes off her and put them on. And long after this was over, I thought about those shoes for years.

Within a few days without any antiseptic to put on my burning face and slashed leg, I began to smell like rotten meat, and I knew I was helpless to save myself. So we knew we had to start to walk somewhere. and I knew it was Laura's shoes that would save me. We didn't know in what direction we should walk, but knew we had to start. Eventually we came to a clearing that was a sweet potato field and we thought we'd found civilization. There was a plane overhead, and we were screaming and waving our arms, till they dipped to let us know they saw us, but they didn't stop. and we figured they were going for help.

    (The sound of dogs barking.)

The sound of wild dogs yipping made us realize they were surrounding us, but it was really humans making the whelping noise. And then they entered the clearing; naked men who looked like they had the largest penises in the world stood before us, but then we realized those huge penises were just protection gourds. It was startling and their dark skin had a shine, which we found out later was from pig fat. Though we didn't know what to make of them, they didn't know what to make of us either. They had never seen people with white skin, and they thought because we were wearing shoes that we had no toes, just hooves. And to add to all this, they believed a legend that the end of the world would come happen when spirits with long hair and light eyes came.

Lt. McCollom commanded us to smile, which we all did, as if we were so happy to see them all. McCollom then held out our candy to them. They looked it over then held out their hands to shake. And then we all stood around and smiled at each other. We had never seen these people and they had never seen us, but it appeared that smiling was universal.

They took us to their huts by a knoll and we had a reception from them the likes we had never seen...Even the Astors' couldn't hold a candle to it. One of the funniest things they did was to blow on our wounds to try to keep our souls from falling out of them. Soon we had no fear at all. And though a plane could not land where we were they were able to send down food for us, and an FM radio. Eventually paratroopers led by Capt. Walter Jr. were able to parachute in.

When they first landed, the tribesman touched them all over, and Capt. Walter Jr. told his men to strip naked so the natives would know they were men. But the truth was the tribe had never seen clothes before as they covered themselves in mud.

Even when I bathed both men and women were fascinated with me. One of the men who I nicknamed Bob Hope began to throw rocks at me, which I found out was a courting ritual. I was even invited into the Queens hut for sweet potatoes, as they were all very friendly and caring. But her husband was also showing interest in me, making the Queen very jealous; that's when things got scary. Other women tried to cut off the tips of my fingers as a punishment. Luckily our men saved me...

After a month the paratroopers and us were finally able to walk through this impenetrable jungle to a place where planes were waiting for us. It was quite the adventure, but not the one I was looking for...I had lost lots of weight; I had chopped off most of my hair because all kinds of jungle tentacles were adhering to it. So when we landed in Australia we were greeted and cheered by citizens and reporters.

"Well Corporal Hastings now that you are back what do you want to do next?" My answer was, "I'd like to shower and have a cold wave."

What started out to be a pleasure trip of much fun, turned into a most unexpected adventure of exploration and survival. Two months later, the war with Japan was over. And I was given an honorary membership of the National World War II Glider Pilots Association. After I got out of the Army, I attended Syracuse University for two years, and I did finally did get married and had two beautiful children, but I was right about not being the marrying kind and was divorced. I moved to Rome, New York and worked at the Griffiss Air Force Base in an administrative position. But my memory of those events come back to me in nightmares and mourning. And sometimes at night when I'm reading or watching television, I think I hear the sound of wild dogs yelping, and I think about Lara's shoes.

Jazzed

Michael Moreth

When You Can Only Proceed by Torch-light

Jennifer M. Phillips

Any fallen evening when the weight
of the bleak world, like wet wool around your shoulders
offers no comfort,

in the very stoop under that weight
pressing your eyes down to the sidewalk's shoulders
where the curb holds back storm-runoff like a fort

by a brown and kelpy tide, stand still and wait.
See, a low light starts caressing the shoulders
of a plantain's leaves in a stone-crack, and there is comfort,

a teaspoonful at a time, a counterweight
of grace, like a dandelion's gold that shoulders
the grass up. See it as scruff, or by blind luck or effort

see it new as ruthless glory, throwing its weight
around the humdrum, lifting off your shoulders
despair's dark, handing you the flashlight of comfort.

Heirloom

Jennifer M. Phillips

You reach an age where you decide to keep
the bowl, broken and reglued, with the one piece
lying in the bottom you can't make fit in again.
From the generation before the last, your not-so-deep
memory curlicues inside it, so it gives ease
of loneliness, like hands clasped in a chain,

reaching down to you. *You belong to us,*
it seems to declare, past worry or question.
You also broken and mended, not quite
entire, the fragments you fret and fuss
trying to incorporate. The generation
after us walks by a different light.

They furnish with small disposables
from Ikea, glass from Pottery Barn. No panic
if a boxful gets smashed or if their tastes change
as they shift across countries. Life is made portable.
They research their genome avidly; how ironic
to be so disinterested in family antiques; how strange

to archive thousands of photos onscreen, with none
offering framed daily greetings from the shelf.
A migrant, I live eye-deep in hand-me-downs
painted, embroidered, given by those who are gone.
Their breakable, graspable love helps compose my self
durable to loss, still willing to break new ground.

All these things will go to strangers, if at all.
Only such stories as I hand on to you,
if they appeal, might linger awhile topside
once I am under the stones. Yet I bless the potter whose tool
and hands shaped this fragile china, orange and blue,
to confide vanished love to me, and from me to you.

Morning's Light

Karen Colstrom

WHO WILL WITNESS FOR THE WITNESS

A one-act play

Susan Hansell

SYNOPSIS

Who Will Witness for the Witness is a lyrical one-act play exploring the lives and the life-outcomes of four fictionalized-yet-factually-based women from Nazi-era Europe as they ponder truth, life, fact, death, and existence.

CHARACTERS*

WOMAN ONE (approx. 20s) plays The Photographer, a fictional composite based on the life of Gerda Taro.

WOMAN TWO (approx. 30s-40s) plays The Philosopher, a fictional composite based on the life of Simone Weil.

WOMAN THREE (approx. late-teens-20s) plays The Spy, a fictional composite based partly on the life of Marthe Cohn.

WOMAN FOUR (approx. 50s-60s) plays The Nun, a fictional composite based on the life of Edith Stein.

*CHARACTERS are historical representations meant to resonate with the current world and may be cast without regard to race/ethnicity or the European period.

SET & TECH (may be achieved as minimally as is necessary)
Moving spots, bare stage, darkness; period gunshots and airplanes; searchlights, barking dogs, wind.

COSTUMING & PROPS (may be achieved as minimally as is necessary)
Clothing approximating Europe c. 1940's; a large book; a rolleiflex camera c. 1935.

MUSIC (optional)
Selections from Franz Schubert's *Winterreise* as sung by Dietrich Fischer-Dieskau in the earliest post-WWII recording with Jorg Demus on piano, as noted in the script.

To LIGHTS UP, PLAY "Der Leiermann/The Organ Grinder" by Franz Schubert as sung by Dietrich Fischer-Dieskau with Jorg Demus on piano.

Enter, WOMAN ONE, as the PHOTOGRAPHER, dressed in rumpled overalls and straw shoes. On a leather strap around her neck is a rolleiflex camera from the

1930s. SHE walks slowly forward, pointing her camera toward the audience while looking down into the view finder.

When she arrives downstage, the PHOTOGRAPHER looks up from her camera without taking a picture.

WOMAN ONE
(as The PHOTOGRAPHER)

I exist.

(WOMAN ONE smiles out to the WORLD.

You exist. We exist.

(The PHOTOGRAPHER looks down into the camera and takes a photograph of the audience.)

(Beat.)

They existed.

(WOMAN ONE shows off her camera.)

This original rolleiflex camera, it exists, shooting big detailed negatives. I make prints and mail them direct to the French dailies from Spain.

(The PHOTOGRAPHER looks down into the camera and takes a series of photographs of the audience, then uses a knob to advance the film.)

(chanting year-dates as she takes photographs)

1934. 1935. 1936.

(Beat.)

I'm not Spanish. Or French. Or even German really, though I was born in Stuttgart.

(Beat.)

My parents came from a place—Galicia—.

(Beat.)

Such a pretty name, Galicia.

(WOMAN ONE chants year-dates as she takes more photographs, turning the knob after each shot.)

1937. 1938. 1939.

(Beat.)

Galicia has a very famous province, a place everyone knows.

(Beat.)

Even if certain types deny knowing.

(Beat.)

We know those types.

>   (The PHOTOGRAPHER points the camera behind her ass, so that her camera points behind her, upstage, and takes a photograph. SHE makes a vulgar raspberry sound.)

>   (Pause.)

Did you know? Before the Germans occupied the infamous province of Galicia, the Russians occupied it first, and the Russians, as the Germans did who came after them— liked to round up bunches of—Poles, Ukrainians, Serbs—anyone who might be considered "illegal"—and put them into camps.

>   (singing year-dates as she takes photographs)

1940. 1941. 1942.

>   (Beat.)

>   (The PHOTOGRAPHER crouches, as if shooting pictures, outside, in a war zone.)

>   (Pause.)

As the Germans advanced, the Russians fled, but first the Russians shot their prisoners.

>   (Beat.)

50,000 dead—found by the Germans upon their arrival.

>   (WOMAN ONE whispers year-dates as she takes photographs, continuing to crouch.)

1943. 1944.

>   (Pause.)

(The PHOTOGRAPHER breaks away for her "job," runs up stage, looks down into her camera, then   looks up, faces forward, then looks down into her camera again, then suddenly turns her camera toward herself, to take a series of "selfies.")

(The CAMERA flashes several times.)

(The PHOTOGRAPHER beams.)

(Beat.)

(WOMAN ONE laughs.)

For all of time. Gerda Taro, that's me. Do you know me? Do you recognize me?

(Beat.)

(The PHOTOGRAPHER places a hand on a hip.)

I'm merely curious. But tell me, have you heard my name?

(Pause.)

Born Gerta Pohorylle, in Stuttgart, 1910. Called Poho by classmates and early friends. Went to France, in 1933, because Germany is already—.

(Beat.)
WOMAN ONE
Left behind two brothers and both parents, who chose to stay, and then — when it was too late to leave—.

(The PHOTOGRAPHER fiddles with her camera.)

And when it's too late to hide, they flee, East, toward — an old idea of home.

(Beat.)

By then East is not such a good direction.

WOMAN ONE, Cont.
(Beat.)

(The PHOTOGRAPHER sighs.)

They survive their capture; even their deportations. To Sajmiste. Another of those someplaces you've heard about, or maybe not heard about. There were so so many! Who can keep track?

(Beat.)

(Enter, from stage right, WOMAN TWO, as THE PHILOSOPHER, carrying an open book.)

(The PHILOSOPHER turns, facing forward, while holding the open book.)

(The PHOTOGRAPHER runs down stage, pivots toward the PHILOSOPHER and snaps pictures.)

WOMAN TWO
(as The PHILOSOPHER)
The Romans killed Archimedes. Afterward, they killed Greece.

(Beat.)

As the Germans, had it not been for England, would have killed France.

(Beat.)

These facts are known. They are facts. There *are* still facts, aren't there?

(answering her own question, with enthusiasm)

Of course, there are!

(Beat.)

WOMAN TWO
Facts can be remembered, written down, studied, understood, and related to deeds, to acts.

(The PHOTOGRAPHER continues snapping a series of pictures of the PHILOSOPHER.)

WOMAN ONE
(to herself, about the photos she's shooting)
Fantastic!

(Beat.)

WOMAN TWO
The Egyptians, for example, believed: No soul can justify itself after death unless it can say, "I never let anyone suffer"; that's a fact; that they believed *this* was what granted a person everlasting joy in the afterworld.

(Enter WOMAN FOUR, as The NUN, from stage left.)

(The NUN crosses herself.)

(The PHOTOGRAPHER moves to snap pictures of The NUN, at first quickly, then more slowly; then, she watches.)

(The NUN and The PHILOSOPHER regard each another with interest, yet from a distance. Without really "seeing" each other, THEY enter into a dialogue. Possibly, THEY talk more to themselves, or, as if to an unseen colleague with whom they are corresponding in letters. THEY walk past each other, yet with each other, and pace and gesture to themselves, and possibly to each other, or to others, seen and unseen.)

WOMAN FOUR
(as The NUN)

I'm eager to know what you will have to say about Heidegger's positive definition of the metaphysical self.

(Beat.)

WOMAN TWO

Holiness is righteousness, and that is a fact.

(Beat.)

WOMAN FOUR

I believe I have the same idea, grounded in philosophy *and* theology.

(Pause.)

WOMAN TWO

The appalling evil in the midst of which we struggle—

(Beat.)

WOMAN FOUR

This phase of life we think of as actual experience—.

(Beat.)

WOMAN TWO

Without even managing to understand how tragic it is—.

(Beat.)

WOMAN FOUR
(mystically)

—Is something momentary.

(Pause.)

Indeed. I have reconciled myself to going beyond—.

(Beat.)

160

WOMAN TWO
(trying to relate)
A rainbow's beautiful semicircle is testimony, that the current phenomena of this world, however terrifying, are subject to limit.

(Pause.)

WOMAN FOUR
About my next book, yes, I do want to tell you, but first—I am ashamed to reveal my rejection from a position in Hamburg, due to the quotas.

(Beat.)

WOMAN TWO
(with fury)
The remedy is to bring back among us the spirit of *truth*.

(Beat.)

WOMAN FOUR
Oh, I find the whole matter funny—but I had hoped the Pope would want to alert the world to what is happening—.

(Beat.)

WOMAN TWO
(still angry)
People talk about punishing the torturers—.

(Beat.)

WOMAN FOUR
(laughing, loudly but shyly)
You must not speak of this "great ontology" of mine, Though I do hope to see it when it's printed.

(Beat.)

(still angry)
But they cannot be punished—.

(Beat.)

WOMAN FOUR
The laws no longer permit me to be in public, as you know. My lectures have been cancelled.

(Beat.)

WOMAN TWO
(with furious concentration)

Only a transformation of the meaning we attach to greatness, from which meaning the torturers must be excluded: That is what they deserve. To be ignored, to be exiled, from the righteous.

(Pause.)

WOMAN FOUR
(with happiness)

Yet... True Being is wisdom *because* it is simple—.

(Beat.)

WOMAN FOUR

—And all mysteries are concealed in it.

(Pause.)

WOMAN TWO

Hitler and his fanatical young followers have never though about *that* as they looked up at the stars at night!

(calmer)

No—. Weakness must not be the servant of force—. Force must be docile to eternal wisdom.

(Beat.)

(The NUN faces forward, still.)

(The PHOTOGRAPHER fiddles with her camera.)

(Long pause.)

WOMAN FOUR

Sunday, August 2nd, 1942—.

(Beat.)

WOMAN TWO
(turning to face forward, along side the NUN)

The meaning of history is up to us.

(Beat.)

WOMAN FOUR

O will to give me / All that leads to you. / O take away from me / All that diverts me from you. / O take me, also, from myself / And give me completely to yourself.

The PHILOSOPHER closes her book and hugs it to her.

(Beat.)

WOMAN FOUR

My sister Rosa and I have been arrested and taken to a barracks in Westerbork.

(Beat.)

We are with two nuns and two Trappist fathers.

(Beat.)

Also Ruth Kantorowitz, Alice Reis, Dr. Meirowsky, two children from the Koningsbosch family.

(Beat.)

The entire Lobe family.

(Pause.)

August 7th—.

(Beat.)

Morning. Still dark.

(Beat.)

We are traveling. East.

(Beat.)

Toward... Galicia?

    (The NUN and the PHILOSOPHER stand, stricken; THEY stare with terror, out and past the audience.)

    (Pause.)

    (Enter, running, from off stage, WOMAN THREE, as The SPY. The SPY runs a few steps, then stops, listening; then SHE runs a few more steps, then SHE stops, listening.)

(The PHOTOGRAPHER runs after her, snapping photographs.)

WOMAN ONE
(happily)

Look! An ordinary girl!

(The NUN looks over at The SPY.)

WOMAN FOUR
(a happy distraction)

Wunderbar!

(The SPY considers running.)

(The SPY takes a few tentative steps.)

(The SPY thinks, then runs like crazy, then stops abruptly, and looks all around.)

(Pause.)

(The SPY falls prone, then crawls, staying close to the ground.)

(Beat.)

(The SPY rolls to her right, then to her left.)

(A hail of GUNFIRE; the sounds of WWII PLANES.)

(The SPY covers her head and waits.)

(The PHOTOGRAPHER snaps pictures.)

(The SPY blinks at the PHOTOGRAPHER, then   stands abruptly, and runs off, stage right.)

(The PHOTOGRAPHER, the NUN and PHILOSOPHER look after theSPY's exit, then look all around, then possibly at each other.)

(The SPY runs back on stage, weaving her way through and around the other WOMEN while she speaks.)

WOMAN THREE
(as The SPY)

Hide? Hide someone? Hide yourself?

(The SPY looks to her left.)

THREE

Walk? Walk to the Post Office, register yourself as required by The Laws?

(The SPY runs a few steps downstage.)

WOMAN THREE

Push, or be pushed! Break, or be broken!

(The SPY runs a few steps upstage.)

If no one's looking? If everyone's looking?

(The SPY runs forward, faces forward, and stands unmoving, breathing heavily. She salutes.)

Marthe Cohn, spy for the Allies. Favorite activity when behind enemy lines?

(Beat.)

Walking with Nazis and listening to them tell each other they can identify Jewish people by their smell!

(The SPY laughs until the NUN, the PHOTOGRAPHER and the PHILOSOPHER join in.)

(THEY ALL laugh until it hurts.)

(Beat.)

(The SPY jumps up and looks to her right.)

WOMAN THREE

Help? Help someone? Help yourself?

(The SPY turns to her right and cups her right hand to her right ear and listens.)

(The SPY turns to her left and cups her left hand to her mouth and stage whispers her code.)

The doctor will come this Monday. The third gate has a new hinge. Bring two bags of bird seed for the parade.

(The SPY dives and rolls then crawls slowly, as if toward enemy lines.)

(The PHOTOGRAPHER trails the SPY.)

(The SPY jumps up and steps forward, and salutes.)

WOMAN THREE

It was I who reported the Siegfried Line had been abandoned. It was I who noted precisely where the fanatical holdouts lay in wait for us in the Black Forest. Ha! We got them.

WOMAN ONE

Ha! She got them!

WOMAN THREE

It was I, decorated with the *Croix de Guerre* for my service with French Intelligence.

(Beat.)

I exist.

WOMAN ONE

She exists!

(The NUN steps forward.)

(Beat.)

WOMAN FOUR

I was. Sister Teresa Benedicta of the Cross.

(Beat.)

Born, Edith Stein, October 12th, 1891, Breslav, Germany.

(Beat.)

WOMAN FOUR

Died, August 9th, 1942.

(Beat.)

Number 44074.

WOMAN ONE
(pointing her camera, excited)

She existed!

WOMAN FOUR
(nods)

I was.

(Beat.)

WOMAN FOUR

Only sorry. Not to be able. To alleviate the suffering. Of those around me. Upon arrival.

WOMAN ONE

Ah! The Arrival. At Auschwitz.

WOMAN ONE, Cont.

(Beat.)

Auschwitz. Once upon a time. A state in a small Kingdom called—*Galicia*.

(Beat.)

Galicia: currently a province in the country called Poland. Birthplace of Copernicus, Chopin, Marie Curie, Catherine the Great, Marcin Gortat, Agnieszka Radwanska, Helena Rubinstein, Schopenhauer, Isaac Bashevis Singer, Billy Wilder.

(Pause.)

(The NUN slaps a yellow star onto her own chest.)

(The PHILOSOPHER slaps a purple triangle onto her own chest.)

(The SPY slaps a red triangle onto her own chest.)

(The PHILOSOPHER slaps a brown triangle onto her chest.)

(The NUN slaps a black triangle onto her chest.)

(The SPY slaps a yellow star onto her chest.)

(The PHILOSOPHER slaps a red triangle onto her chest.)

(The SPY slaps a brown triangle onto her chest.)

(The PHILOSOPHER slaps a yellow star onto her chest.)

(The NUN slaps a red triangle onto her chest.)

(Pause.)

(The NUN, the SPY, and the PHILOSOPHER face forward as if taking mug-shots. The PHOTOGRAPHER runs up to take each shot.)

(The NUN, the SPY, and the PHILOSOPHER face profile. The PHOTOGRAPHER takes a shot of each profile.)

(Pause.)

(In a sudden frenzy, The PHILOSOPHER, The SPY, and The NUN slap patches of different colors and symbols [yellow triangles, green triangles, black triangles, pink triangles, red bars, green bars, blue bars, purple bars, pink bars, black bars, brown bars, black circle targets, red circle targets, etc.—in different combinations and positions] onto themselves and onto each other, all over their bodies.)

(A choice can be made to add current social epithets, in one or two word descriptors, as badges, onto the ACTORS' garments, such as "immigrant," "inferior," "insane," etc. as a contemporary resonance; this choice is entirely optional.)

(When THE NUN, THE SPY and THE PHILOSOPHER stop, they are breathing hard.)

(THEY look at each other, and move apart, to recover themselves.)

(The PHOTOGRAPHER takes pictures of their terror, shame, guilt.)

(Beat.)

(The PHOTOGRAPHER pivots away suddenly and waves out toward the audience.)

(Beat.)

WOMAN ONE

Gerda Taro here, the photojournalist; remember me?

(Beat.)

WOMAN ONE

For the record, I died on July 26, 1937, while covering the Spanish Civil War. By accident, I was hit by a tank. Can you believe it?

(in disbelief)

Me! With my work, throughout Europe, in newspapers, in magazines!

(to herself)

What a waste.

(Beat.)

But listen: For the purposes of this story, technically, I'm dead. Truthfully, I didn't live to see any of this.

(Beat.)

I confess, the future makes me—*uncomfortable.*

(WOMAN ONE laughs, uncomfortably.)

(After a beat, the PHILOSOPHER raises her hand, as if she wants to be called on, as if in a classroom.)

WOMAN TWO

Simone Weil, here. Author, mystic. Born in France, February 3rd, 1909. Died in August of
1943. While working in England, for MI6.

 (Beat.)

WOMAN TWO

Also technically dead, though not *uncomfortably* so.

 (The PHILOSOPHER smiles. The NUN nods and shares in the PHILOSOPHER's
 smile; perhaps the two of them share a rueful laugh.)

WOMAN FOUR

Here we are.

 (Beat.)

WOMAN TWO

In this history. We exist.

WOMAN ONE

Wait! Did you know? My funeral was a procession of thousands through the streets of
Paris.

 (Beat.)

And because I was famous, my family would learn of my death — while I would never
learn—.

WOMAN TWO

We know.

WOMAN THREE

We understand.

WOMAN ONE

—Of theirs.

WOMAN FOUR

We must—.

WOMAN THREE

—Go forward.

 (Beat.)

 (The PHOTOGRAPHER fiddles with her camera, procrastinating.)

(WOMAN TWO, WOMAN THREE and WOMAN FOUR watch WOMAN ONE,
waiting.)

WOMAN ONE

Did you know Joel Meyerowitz will use a large-view camera like this one to take his photos of the World Trade Center ruins?

(Beat.)

The detail, the scope—is the best for seeing into.

(Beat.)

What we don't want to see.

(Beat.)

WOMAN THREE

Don't you see?

WOMAN FOUR

It's time.

WOMAN TWO

We've arrived.

(The NUN, the SPY, the PHILOSOPHER and the PHOTOGRAPHER join hands,
facing forward.)

WOMAN ONE

Where are we?

WOMAN FOUR

This place.

WOMAN THREE

The gates.

WOMAN TWO

The tracks.

(Together, the FOUR WOMEN take a step forward.)

WOMAN ONE

There's a building.

WOMAN FOUR

Guards.

                    WOMAN TWO
                    (shouting)
To the left! To the right!

(The FOUR WOMEN take a step forward.)

                    WOMAN TWO
                    (even louder)
To the left! To the right!

(THE FOUR WOMEN take a step forward.)

                    WOMAN ONE
                    (a shout)
Farther.

                    WOMAN FOUR
                    (a prayer)
Further.

                    WOMAN THREE
                    (overlapping with below)
Un—fathomable.

                    WOMAN TWO
                    (overlapping after "un")
Un—fathomable.

                    WOMAN FOUR
                    (overlapping with the above))
Un—fathomable.

                    WOMAN ONE
                    (overlapping with the above))
Un—fathomable.

(Pause.)

(Then: SEARCHLIGHTS. Barking DOGS.)

(A long cold WIND.)

(The FOUR WOMEN take a step forward.)

                    WOMAN ONE
Yet, it did happen.

                    WOMAN TWO
That's a fact.

WOMAN FOUR

Was I alone?

WOMAN TWO

We were together.

WOMAN THREE

On the right?

WOMAN ONE

On the left?

WOMAN FOUR

I was first in line.

WOMAN TWO

I was last in line.

WOMAN THREE

I spoke up.

WOMAN ONE

I stayed quiet.

WOMAN TWO

I fought back.

WOMAN FOUR

Some collaborated.

WOMAN THREE

Not me!

WOMAN TWO

On the left!

WOMAN ONE

On the right!

WOMAN FOUR

Some gave a hand.

WOMAN THREE

A foot.

WOMAN TWO

Early.

WOMAN ONE

Late.

WOMAN FOUR

Near.

WOMAN THREE

Far.

WOMAN ONE

An inch.

WOMAN FOUR

An instant.

WOMAN TWO

An alley.

WOMAN THREE

A door.

    (Long pause.)

WOMAN ONE

Was this our choice?

WOMAN FOUR

We made our choices.

WOMAN THREE

From the choices we had.

WOMAN TWO

Tiny baby choices.

WOMAN THREE

There was *no* choice.

WOMAN FOUR

There was *one* choice.

WOMAN ONE

I *had* no choice.

WOMAN TWO

Sometimes. That's the choice we have.

    (Pause.)

                              WOMAN THREE
Let's remember.

                              WOMAN ONE
The facts.

                              WOMAN THREE
The righteous facts.

                              WOMAN TWO
Beautiful facts.

                              WOMAN ONE
Ugly facts.

                              WOMAN FOUR
Our beautiful truth.

      (Beat.)

                              WOMAN TWO
Our lives.

                              WOMAN ONE
Ourselves.

                              WOMAN FOUR
Our love.

                              WOMAN THREE
Of justice.

      (Still holding hands, the FOUR WOMEN now drop hands, turn together, and walk
      straight upstage, side-by-side.)

      (THEY stand in a line, with their backs to the audience. They stretch their arms out
      from their sides, not quite touching, or just barely touching, each other's hands.
      This should look something like PAPER-DOLLS.)

      (BACK-LIGHTING will accentuate this PAPER-DOLL effect, effectively
      SILHOUETTING the FOUR WOMEN.)

      (TABLEAU.)

      (Then, loud-whispering.)

                              WOMAN TWO
I existed.

WOMAN ONE

We existed.

WOMAN FOUR

They existed.

WOMAN THREE

She existed.

(The FOUR WOMEN now drop their arms and turn to face forward.)

(THEY stand in a line, facing the audience.)

WOMAN THREE

I exist.

WOMAN TWO

She exists.

WOMAN ONE

We exist.

WOMAN FOUR

They exist.

(Beat.)

ALL FOUR WOMEN TOGETHER

You.

(Beat.)

Exist.

(TABLEAU.)

BLACKOUT.

PLAY "Mut!/Courage" by Franz Schubert as sung by Dietrich Fischer-Dieskau with Jorg Demus on piano.

END OF PLAY.

Old House

Mark Clarke

Deciduous

Rosalie Hendon

From Latin, *deciduus*: tending to fall

Like a candle and its flame,
the trees begin to turn.
From the top down:
Maples with wine colored leaves
The hackberry in the next yard
vibrating with chartreuse.
The honeyed tones of the honey locust,
gold against the sky.
Redbud's hearts, sunshine bright.

What we see is a conservation of resources,
a storing away for winter.
Alchemy, turning sunlight to sugar.
Precious chlorophyll is siphoned back,
a green retreat.
In its wake, leaves are colorful, expendable.
Ready to fall.

Through the frosts and freezes
and snow lashing branches,
ice hanging and cracking and thawing,
they endure.

Trees remind us:
Shed what you don't need.
Hold close what is precious.
Believe in spring.

Dream Journal #15 (Plum Armchair)

Rosalie Hendon

I should have known better than to touch that old armchair.
I rested my hand on its plum velvet anyway.
An iron pin sprouted from my fingertip
(left hand, index finger).
I raised it, surprised to see metal in my skin.
You smiled at me, shaking your head.
Gently, you pulled out the startling length of it.
I felt no pain.
Watched as red filled in the hole.

I should thank you, but somehow
all I can think is that
you took something from me
and left me with nothing.

Barn

Mark Clarke

DANIEL LAID TO REST

A One-Act Play

William Robert Carey

SYNOPSIS
SHUKO and her son DAN-O are attending the funeral of DANIEL MAMMEN, former lover to SHUKO and father to DAN-O. While they wait for other attendees, the deceased's estranged transgender daughter, DANIELLE, arrives and tells them about her troubled relationship with MAMMEN and her struggle to become her true self.

CHARACTERS
SHUKO, late 30s Asian-American woman, a single mother attending the funeral of her late lover.
DAN-O, 19-year-old American man attending the funeral of his father.
DANIELLE, 30-something trans woman attending the funeral of her father.

LIGHTS UP ON
SETTING
A funeral parlor with chairs and a casket.

SHUKO and DAN-O sit together. She is prim and erect; he is checking his phone. After a few moments, SHUKO looks at her watch.

DAN-O

No one's coming, Mom.

SHUKO

You don't know that.

DAN-O

People hate him.

SHUKO

They don't hate him.

DAN-O

Like a leper they do.

SHUKO

Please don't talk about your father like that.

                                        DAN-O
Even his friends aren't here. They're all pussies.

                                        SHUKO
They're not...

        (sighs)

Okay.

                                        DAN-O
Fair weather friends.

                                        SHUKO
Way of the world, honey.

                                        DAN-O
But even his law partner?

                                        SHUKO
Bob McDougall.

                                        DAN-O
Bob McDouchbag.

                                        SHUKO
He couldn't come if he wanted to, honey. Felons can't consort with felons.

                                        DAN-O
Dad's dead, Mom. He's unconsortable.

        (SHUKO shrugs.)

                                DAN-O, Con't
Didn't dad help him get started as a lawyer?

                                        SHUKO
                                        (nodding)
And finished.

                                        DAN-O
It wasn't Dad's fault the Feds went after him too. He should be here.

                                        SHUKO
Jail changes people, dear. Makes them bitter.

                                        DAN-O
It was sure hard on Dad.

                              SHUKO
Crushed him.

                              DAN-O
Sometimes, when we were alone, he would hug me and say I was the only child he had left.
And then he'd start crying.

        (shaking his head)

I didn't know what to...to say, you know?

        (SHUKO nods.)

                         DAN-O, Cont'd
He has another son, doesn't he?

                              SHUKO
                            (nodding)
Two. One died. He hasn't seen the other in years. That's what he meant. He has a lot of
guilt about him. Both of them. It ate at him. And your father wasn't the same after prison.

                              DAN-O

The twitching was the worst. Hard to look at.

        (SHUKO nods.)

                         DAN-O, Cont'd
But in some ways, he was better. Not as hot-headed. He seemed angry a lot when I was
growing up. Like that time he lost his shit on Christmas, arguing with Uncle Tim about
something stupid.

                              SHUKO
The Beatles.

                              DAN-O
That's it. Freaked me out. Especially since I thought they were arguing about bugs.

                              SHUKO
Nobody could tell your father anything about music.

                              DAN-O
That's weird, 'cause he wasn't exactly plugged in. Did you ever look at his record collection?
It's all sixty years old.

                              SHUKO
Some older.

                              DAN-O
And nothing but jazz -- by dudes I never heard of. He made me listen to some of it once. It
was brutal. How did people party to that crap?

                              SHUKO
                            (shrugs)
Don't ask me. I was into Madonna and Tears For Fears.

                              DAN-O
I know. I listened to one of your old mix tapes once. What a trip. Janet Jackson and Mariah
Carey. I almost lost my lunch. And what's with MC Hammer? That was some potato quality
shit.

                              SHUKO
It was good for dancing.

                              DAN-O
It was like havin' your ears roto-rootered. But Pop's was worse.

                              SHUKO
At least it gave him pleasure at the end.

                              DAN-O
He was groovin' on it all right. I caught him air-saxing once. He just looked at me and
smiled. Didn't miss a beat.

                              SHUKO
Before you were born, he took me to some jazz lounges. I pretended to like it. Made him
happy. When he was young, he wanted to be a musician. His father pushed him into law.

                              DAN-O
That sure worked out well.

                              SHUKO
It did for us, honey. If he hadn't become a lawyer and judge, I wouldn't have met him, and
you wouldn't be here. He took good care of us. His mother, too. People want to paint him
one color, but he had a lot of different sides. Everybody makes compromises.

                              DAN-O
I guess you gotta be lucky enough to skate on the bad ones.

        (DANIELLE enters in a stylish black dress.)

                            SHUKO, Cont'd
Oh, look. Someone's here.

        (standing)

Hello. Please, come in.

DANIELLE
(glancing around)

I'm not too late, am I?

SHUKO
No, no, please. You're very welcome. I'm Shuko Gish and...

(She pats DAN-O's arm, and he stands.)

...this is my son, Danny.

DANIELLE
I'm Danielle Mamm. Are you the only ones here?

SHUKO

Afraid so.

DANIELLE
What about his wife, Fabiana?

(SHUKO shakes her head.)

DANIELLE, Cont'd
Is she alright?

SHUKO
Yes, uhm...well, yes and no. She and Dan had a falling out before he died.

DANIELLE
Really? What happened?

SHUKO
That's hard to explain.

DAN-O
The bitch killed him.

DANIELLE
What?

SHUKO
No, no, that's not exactly true. Dan was already in a coma. But that's what the police think.

DANIELLE
Why?

DAN-O
She had her hands around his throat when he died.

                              DANIELLE
Oh my God.

                              SHUKO
She kind of flipped out in the hospital room.

                              DANIELLE
Why?

                              SHUKO
She found out about me.

                              DAN-O
And me.

                              SHUKO
When we visited him.

                              DAN-O
She went totally bitchcakes.

                              SHUKO
So we don't expect to see her.

                              DAN-O
And we'll run if we do.

                              DANIELLE
Is she in jail?

                              SHUKO
Posted bail, I think. But she's going to need a good lawyer.

                              DANIELLE
                          (looking at casket)
Too bad Dad is dead.

                              DAN-O
One of the downsides of killing him.

                              SHUKO
Excuse me, did you call him Dad?

        (DANIELLE nods.)

                              SHUKO, Cont'd
I wasn't aware he had a daughter.

DANIELLE

He wasn't either. I played his son for a while. People called me Daniel then.

SHUKO

Oh my God. You're Danny Mammen?

DAN-O

Holy shit.

SHUKO

Excuse me. I didn't mean to sound... It's just such a surprise. When did you...you know...?

DANIELLE

Transition? People ask me that all the time. It's hard to explain. There wasn't a big, *voila*, "I am woman" moment, you know? It was more like a lot of big and small decisions over time. Even after surgery, there was an acclimation period, physical and psychological; plus, I had to get used to the transphobia. And the threats. Not that you get used to that. But if you're asking when I converted to Danielle, that was about 10 years ago.

DAN-O

Does that mean you don't have a schwanz?

SHUKO
(slapping his arm)

Danny!

DAN-O

What? She brought it up.

DANIELLE

I don't recall any phallic references, but if you must know, my equipment is fully updated.

DAN-O

Cool.

DANIELLE

But that's not the measure of a man. Or a woman, for that matter. We're more *a posteriori* than *a priori*.

DAN-O

What?

DANIELLE

The schwanz isn't everything. We're the sum of many parts.

SHUKO

Like your name. You changed it. Even the last one.

                    DANIELLE
                    (nodding)
When I became Danielle, I didn't want to be Mammen anymore.

                    SHUKO
Because your father went to prison?

                    DANIELLE
God no. I changed it long before that. I wanted something feminine to go with Danielle. I considered Pearl and Grace--'cause they're soft and lovely, you know? Then I imagined myself dark and mysterious. That's when Raven made a strong run. And Slayer--an homage to Buffy the Vampire Slayer.

                    DAN-O
She was hot.

                    DANIELLE
Yes, she was. But I got over that. Then it occurred to me that Mamm is the first syllable of my last name. What's more feminine than Mamm?

                    DAN-O
Doll?

                    DANIELLE
Hm. Danielle Doll. I like the alliteration, but it's a little stripper-ish. And Mamm is part of my birth name. It feels organic.

                    DAN-O
You're Miss Mamm! What a riot!

                    DANIELLE
And it's funny--who knew? But enough about me. How do you know Dad?

                    SHUKO
Well, that's a long story.

                    DAN-O
He's my dad, too.

                    DANIELLE
What? You're...you're kidding?

        (DAN-O shakes his head.)

                    DANIELLE, Cont'd
Oh my God.

        (to SHUKO)

DANIELLE, Cont'd
Then you're his...? I don't want to use the wrong word.

SHUKO
(shrugging)
I've never found a good one.

DANIELLE
Roomie doesn't quite cut it, does it?

SHUKO
No.

DANIELLE
How about non-traditional family ladylove?

DAN-O
What a mouthful.

SHUKO
I'll take it.

DANIELLE
How long have you known Dad?

SHUKO
About twenty-two years.

DANIELLE
(staggered)
Twenty-two!

SHUKO
Are you okay?

DANIELLE
I'm...I'm just...shocked.

SHUKO
Do you need some water?

DANIELLE
I need nitroglycerin.

(DANIELLE finds a chair and sits. They sit beside her.)

DANIELLE, Cont'd
Let me see if I've got this straight. It sounds like you and Dad got together around the same time Dad and Fabiana got married.

                         SHUKO
                      (grimacing)
The timing wasn't ideal.

                        DANIELLE
That was right after my mother died. And I ran away.

                         DAN-O
Why'd you run away?

                        DANIELLE
Oh, well, that's, uh...

      (sighs)

A lot of reasons. Mom was gone. Dad and I weren't getting along. He was always working
on me. Pushing me into football and boxing and baseball.

                         SHUKO
He told me you were good at baseball.

                        DANIELLE
I was alright. A good fielder. Fair hitter. But all that dirt and sweat? Eech. And what's with
the spitting? It's disgusting.

                         DAN-O
They grab their peckers a lot too.

                        DANIELLE
More of the phallus.

                         SHUKO
He's nineteen.

                         DAN-O
And a Cub's fan. Don't start baggin' on them.

                         SHUKO
So, you left because Dan was pushing you into sports?

                        DANIELLE
No. Though football almost killed me. If I had an ounce of macho that knocked it out of me.
But the bridge too far was when he sent me to Pray Gay Away camp.

                         DAN-O
Pray Gay Away? That's hysterical.

                              DANIELLE
Not so much.

                               DAN-O
Why? Too much praying?

                              DANIELLE
Too much everything. There were about 25 men at the retreat. I was one of the youngest.
At the orientation, a pastor stood on a stage and railed about the homosexual lifestyle. He
said God created everyone heterosexual, but demons planted wicked thoughts in people's
heads to make them turn gay, leading to disease, depravity, and misery. While he talked,
they projected gay lifestyle pictures on a screen. Most of the people looked like drug
addicts, but some of the pictures were kind of erotic, which confused me. At the end, he
urged us to work on our masculinity and buddied us up with hyper-heteros.

                               SHUKO
What are those?

                              DANIELLE
Super masculine guys. Mine was tall, blond, and athletic -- pretty hot actually, which
confused me again. His name was Josh Armstrong. I always wondered if it was his real
name. He usually had a toothpick in his mouth and, whenever he lectured me, he'd put a
foot up on a chair like he was doing a Harley Davidson commercial. On the second day, he
took me to a Target to buy blue jeans and Henley shirts. I think I got a shirt for every day of
the week. He threw away my penny-loafers and made me wear Chuka boots. I was afraid he
was going to make me buy a gun. After that, we worked on man spreading. I had to sit like
this all the time. Whenever I crossed my legs, he'd slap my knee. It really conditioned me. I
didn't stop sitting like this until I started wearing dresses.

                               DAN-O
I can't stand sitting with my legs crossed. It crushes my junk.

        (Beat.)
                               DAN-O
What? It does.

        (He crosses his legs and grimaces.)

Ugh.

                              DANIELLE
Anyway, on the fourth day they took me to electroconvulsive therapy.

        (SHUKO shakes her head.)

                          DANIELLE, Cont'd
It's basically electroshock therapy. They showed me homosexual movies and zapped me
with electricity during sex scenes.

SHUKO

It sounds like something out of a "Clockwork Orange."

DANIELLE

It's probably where they got the idea. Original thinking wasn't their métier. The next day they gave me nausea-inducing drugs and showed me more gay movies. After that there were a lot of cold showers, holy-roller books, and praying the gay away. They tried hypnosis, too, but I wasn't a good subject for that.

DAN-O

Doesn't look like you were a good subject for any of it.

DANIELLE

Nobody is. It just screws with your head. It made me think I was ugly and evil. I considered killing myself.

SHUKO

No.

DANIELLE
(nodding)

But I never got close. I couldn't figure out how to do it. I hate heights, so jumping off a building was out. I don't like the sight of blood, so I couldn't cut my wrists. Pills seemed like the best bet, but I was afraid I'd get sick and throw up. Then, around that time I went to a party with an older guy I knew, Benedict, who was twenty. When we walked into the apartment, the first thing I saw was a tall slim woman standing in the center of the room with a bunch of guys. She looked amazing, with long blond hair and a low-cut lavender blouse. I couldn't take my eyes off her. She seemed to glow. Benedict saw me staring at her and said, "You like that, don't you?" I wasn't sure how to respond. I mean, I was fascinated, but not attracted. So, I said, "She's beautiful." And Benedict says, "Yeah. Except she's not a she. She's a he." She was a pre-op trans. I was flabbergasted. I had never known anyone like her. Benedict said her name was Aurora and she performed in gay clubs. Later, when I was alone, she spotted me staring at her and came over. I nearly had a heart attack. I thought she was mad because I was staring. But she introduced herself and said, "You're intrigued, aren't you? But you don't know why. And that's okay. You'll figure it out. And when you do, never be ashamed of who you are. Never be afraid to be your full self. In the meantime, remember, chaos gives birth to shimmering stars." Then she kissed me and walked away. I was so overwhelmed I almost cried. I felt like something had been released inside me. I realized people were trying to change me into something I wasn't. From something I wasn't. How crazy is that? I couldn't let that go on anymore. I was who I was. I needed to be that. To love that. And people needed to accept it.

SHUKO

So, you ran away?

(DANIELLE nods.)

SHUKO

Where did you go?

DANIELLE

San Francisco. Then LA. I got a degree in psychotherapy at UCLA.

SHUKO

Wow. How did you pay for it?

DANIELLE

Worked odd jobs in stores and coffee shops. I did some stripping. Gay clubs at first, then transgender. I did what I had to do. And I met a lot of interesting people. People who were smiling and dancing and celebrating who they were--flowering under God's glare. I realized I wanted that. It helped me figure out who I was. For years, I thought I was gay and felt bad about it--and it wasn't even true. It took me a long time to realize I was a woman trying to get out of a man's body.

SHUKO

And you had to get away from Dan to do that?

DANIELLE

After Gay Away, I could never be sure what he'd do to me.

        (feeling emotional, she sighs)

Sorry. I haven't talked about this in a while.

SHUKO

You sure you wouldn't like a glass of water?

DANIELLE

Not nearly strong enough.

DAN-O

There's a bar around the corner. We could go. Not much happenin' here.

DANIELLE

Not for you maybe.

        (to SHUKO)

Are there more of him?

SHUKO

Two girls.

DANIELLE

Oh my God! I have sisters?

        (SHUKO nods.)

                              DANIELLE
That's... How old are they?

                              SHUKO
Ten. They're twins.

                              DANIELLE
Twins! I have twin sisters! Unbelievable. What are their names?

                              SHUKO
Grace and Hope.

                              DANIELLE
Grace! That's a name I considered.

          (SHUKO nods and smiles. DANIELLE laughs, enjoying the moment.)

                              DANIELLE
          (looking at DAN-O)

And you. You're my brother.

                              DAN-O
Pretty wild, huh?

                              DANIELLE
                              (nodding)
I'm sorry. I forgot your name.

                              DAN-O
Daniel. But my friends call me Dan-O. You know, like *Hawaii 5-O*.

          (He mimics the tv show theme song.)

                              DANIELLE
                              (laughing)
I get it. But your real name is Daniel? After Dad?

                              DAN-O
Daniel J. Mammen the Third.

                              DANIELLE
The Third?

                              DAN-O
Yeah.

                              DANIELLE
No.

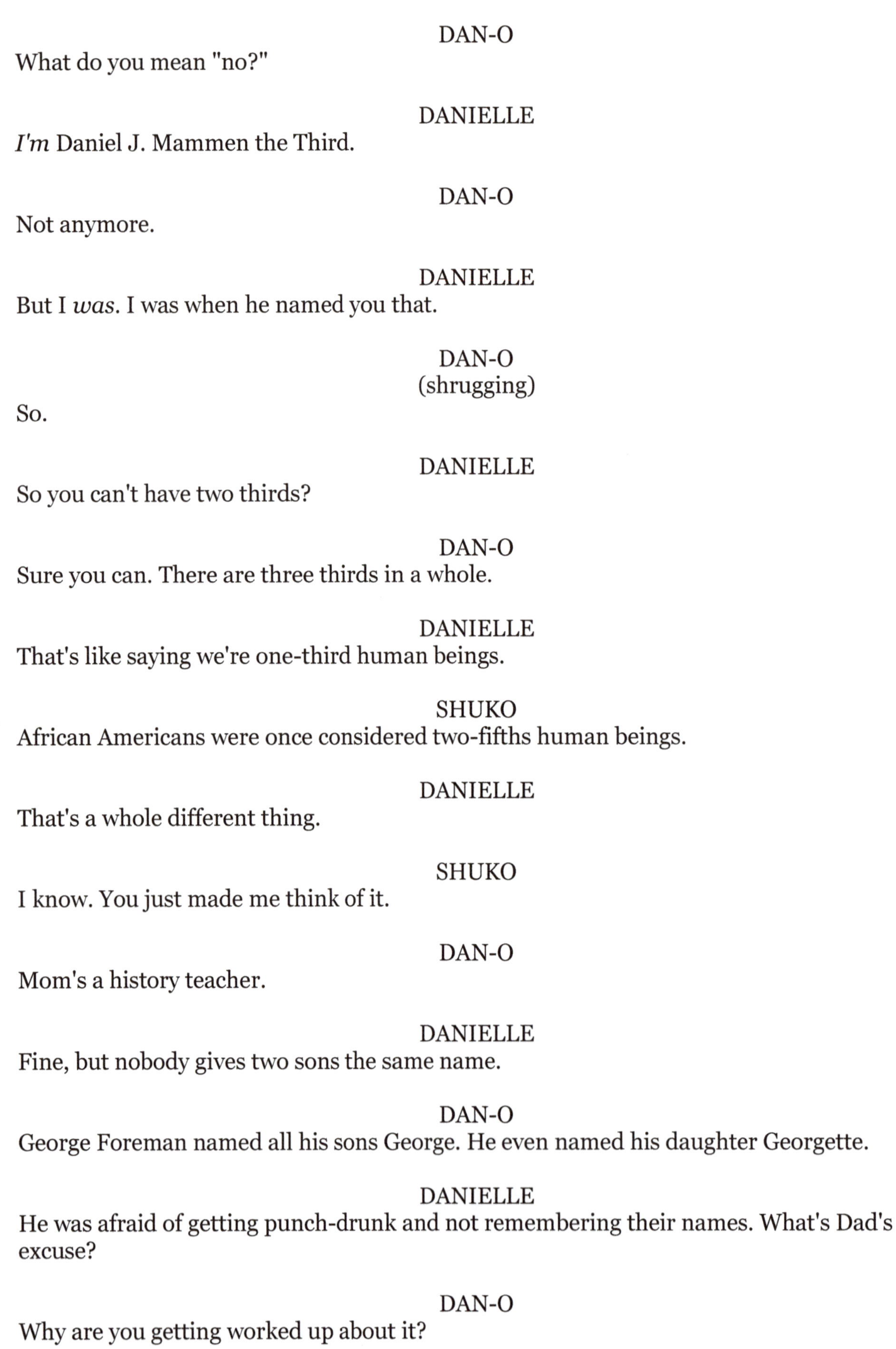

                              DAN-O
What do you mean "no?"

                            DANIELLE
I'm Daniel J. Mammen the Third.

                              DAN-O
Not anymore.

                            DANIELLE
But I *was*. I was when he named you that.

                              DAN-O
                           (shrugging)
So.

                            DANIELLE
So you can't have two thirds?

                              DAN-O
Sure you can. There are three thirds in a whole.

                            DANIELLE
That's like saying we're one-third human beings.

                             SHUKO
African Americans were once considered two-fifths human beings.

                            DANIELLE
That's a whole different thing.

                             SHUKO
I know. You just made me think of it.

                              DAN-O
Mom's a history teacher.

                            DANIELLE
Fine, but nobody gives two sons the same name.

                              DAN-O
George Foreman named all his sons George. He even named his daughter Georgette.

                            DANIELLE
He was afraid of getting punch-drunk and not remembering their names. What's Dad's
excuse?

                              DAN-O
Why are you getting worked up about it?

DANIELLE

Because he gave you *my name*.

DAN-O

But you're not using it anymore.

DANIELLE

Yes, but...I don't know, it just... It's a shock, that's all. You think you have a name, an identity, and you find it's fungible. That *you're* fungible.--But you're right. You're absolutely right. I don't use it. I don't need it. It's all yours. You are forever the one and only Daniel J. Mammen the Third.

SHUKO

Hopefully.

    (DANIELLE and DAN-O look at her.)

SHUKO, Cont'd

As far as I know. But Dan had so many secrets. From so many people. Maybe even me. I never felt like I completely knew him.

    (DANIELLE nods. She gets up and walks over to the casket. SHUKO and DAN-O follow and stand beside her.

DANIELLE

You suppose he ever figured it out for himself?

SHUKO

He tried. In prison, he had a lot of time to think.

DANIELLE

What a place for him to end up. Who would've thought?

SHUKO

He was still trying to get his conviction overturned right up to the end. It drove him crazy that he was convicted of a crime he didn't commit.

DAN-O

Yeah, that sucks.

DANIELLE

It's not like he was *innocent*.

DAN-O

But he didn't take bribes. That's the point.

                              DANIELLE

But he cheated on his taxes for years. That's where the money came from, not bribes. He
should have told the Feds that.

                               DAN-O

He still would have gone to jail.

                              DANIELLE

Yes. That's the point. It's a dyadic completion -- a balancing of debts and penance.

                               DAN-O

If you're a philosophy major.

                               SHUKO

Why did you come here after so many years?

                              DANIELLE

He was my father. I can change a lot of things, but not that. I wish I had come sooner.
Maybe we could have looked into each other's eyes and seen who we really were for once.

     (Beat.)

                               DAN-O

Maybe you did in a parallel universe. Maybe there's an alternate reality where he was a
musician, and you were a girl, and everything was awesome.

                              DANIELLE

So, I'm what in this adaptation, the daughter of a starving musician?

                               DAN-O

Yeah, but it's cool because he smokes dope all the time.

                              DANIELLE

And how do you fit into this scenario?

                               DAN-O

Nowhere. Mom hooks up with Brat Pitt, and I'm a made man.

                              DANIELLE

Dan-O paradise.

                               DAN-O

The yin to our yang. If only universes collided.

                              DANIELLE

I think they have.

          (DANIELLE walks back to a chair and sits. DAN-O and SHUKO join her.)

DANIELLE, Cont'd
How much longer are visiting hours.

SHUKO
(checking her watch)
About 45 minutes.

DANIELLE
I'll wait with you.

(SHUKO nods. Beat.)

SHUKO
Are you coming to the graveside services?

DANIELLE
I hadn't thought about it. Do you want me to?

SHUKO
I think it would be nice. Don't you think it would be nice, Danny?

DAN-O
Sure. It's not like the limo's gonna be crowded.

SHUKO
You could come to the house afterward. Meet your sisters.

DANIELLE
Really?

(SHUKO nods.)

DANIELLE, Cont'd
I'd like that. I really would.

(Beat.)

SHUKO
Did you know Dan left 25% of his estate to you?

(DANIELLE nods.)

SHUKO, Cont'd
I think he wanted you to be happy.

DANIELLE
(nodding)
I suppose he did. In his way.

(SFX: A saxophone plays a wistful song. A light comes up on a silhouette of DANIEL MAMMEN playing the sax.)

Lights fade on DANIELLE, SHUKO and DAN-O, and then MAMMEN.

BLACK OUT.

THE END

River Sky—Glorious Morning

Roberta I. Mayes

What Happens When You Fail Us

Ruth J. Heflin

One poet pulls his poem at the actual
last minute, which costs us time and money.

We are not rich, not spoiled by excesses.
Yet we yearn for beauty, strive to make each
publication glorious, worthy of every coffee table
for every waiting room in the world,
something every person is attracted to so will
want to read, to gaze at its images, to live
in its stories, essays, one-act plays,
screenplays, poetry, and art.

So, when even just one poet pulls his one poem
from our publication at the literal last minute,
his callous disregard for our welfare costs us deeply.
Hours will have to be spent editing the magazine,
Again, to remove the one poem, the writer's biography,
their mentions on the two Contents pages,
his name from the back of the carefully crafted cover,
created to exacting standards by our printer,
which will take so much time to remake for the whole
Magazine just to remove that one name

At the last minute...

simply because one writer forgot to tell another publisher
his work was already accepted for publication
by us, failed to do
"the cold hard math"
that his lack of communication
created,

Not understanding that we do all this out of our love
for art, literature, and other writers, but that
we cannot live on good wishes alone.

And for My Next Trick, I Relive My Past Trauma for the Poem

Kait Quinn

I lie fetaled on top of the buttercream
white Holiday Inn comforter, next to a man who's getting married
tomorrow, until my feet get hotel-AC-in-July frigid and my body

betrays me, joins groom under cover of cotton and down.
I keep my thighs sealed, back turned, knees married like opposite
poles of a magnet, and still his fingers march up

my hip, down my gusset. Tomorrow he'll walk up a crimson
aisle, promise fidelity to his bride's face before her mother, father,
God. She'll cellophane and blue box her ivory gown—birth of a family

heirloom—while I hold a wake for my bare legs, vow never
to wear a dress near a man again. I toss this one like a wilted
marigold bouquet into the trash bin when I get home, hide my

hamstrings from the sun for over a decade. Can you see monkshood
and delphinium blossom between tendon and bone? Ghosts
that haunt these limbs anemic? I bet she takes out her unaged

dress for the kids' *oooh*s and *aaah*s. Bet he's never detailed to her the satin
of my dryer-dulled hipsters, the unraveled bow, hole in the lace. Never
thinks of me, a whole bed and two more feet away from my partner,

whose gentle, untarnished hands I furl against.

The World's My Stage

Karen Colstrom

Spring

Kait Quinn

Mom dresses us in blue jeans
and white blouses, drives 290 halfway
to Bastrop just to get our annual
bluebonnet and Indian paintbrush
portraits. After the camera's packed
away, sister's fever spikes. I vomit
chocolate milk and charcuterie
sausage all over the front seat.
Mom pulls over to wet wipe the console,
the dashboard; strips me down, swaddles
my sticky torso in a charcoal wolf
t-shirt we're not sure is dirty or
clean but at least doesn't smell
like puke. I dress myself

in black for my granddad's funeral.
I'm nineteen and broke. The only black
dress I own is the one Mom bought
me at fifteen for the Sophomore Girls dance.
The diamond-shaped silver
sequin patch gathering obsidian
chiffon at the waist—just the right amount
of cheap glitz for a conference room
floor discoed with drunk teenagers—
feels gaudy in the episcopal church,
at the edge of Granddad's grave.

Three years later, I'll bury a saffron
and marigold dress under coffee grounds
and bar receipts. Because all that color
will just remind me of crashing a three-star
hotel bachelor party, too drunk
to stop the groom's hand slipping up
the bouquet of my skirt, across cotton
gusset, trampling me wilted as California's
super blooms crushed by influencers
for the 'gram.

Now April comes awash in magenta
and daffodil, and I drown my limbs
in a deluge of oversized sweatpants,

(no stanza break)

X-large men's t-shirts dyed in various shades
of overcast. I flood the peonies
and hydrangeas in onyx. Uproot
every garden from my closet. Set every
above-the-knee dress on fire. Never
effloresce from the ash.

Ode to the Neighborhood Swimming Pool

Kait Quinn

I cling to the curved cement edge
while my sister practices underwater
handstand origami with her legs, takes
a beluga-sized breath to carry her

all twelve feet down to slap palm
to square vent. Count to three.
Get the hair wet. If you scream underwater
do you make a sound? I breech the gauzy

surface with pink, needle eyes and water
up my nose but a little more fearless.
Give me Pop Rocks. Give my olfactory
epithelium a flood of chlorine and ten

different brands of sunscreen. Give us fifty cents
to split a coke we sip and pass between
our avobenzone, sweat sticky bodies
draped on Princess Jasmine and *Lion King*

beach towels—sister's limbs bronzing,
mine ripening like a chilled cherry no matter
how much Banana Boat I slather on.
We work up an appetite for microwaved

hot dogs and box mac 'n cheese
doggy paddling the deep end, inhaling sun
and chemical, blistering our feet on grouted
pebble, counting how many tip toes

we can bounce down the slope from
three feet to four feet to five before
we have no choice but to flex our lungs,
measure survival in seconds.

Hidalgo

Michael Moreth

GOD DAMN DOG

Excerpted scenes from the screenplay

Cid Andrenelli

SYNOPSIS

God Damn Dog is a drama following the lives of a multi generational Iranian family living in exile in the West. When the story starts, the children, playing outside, witness the mother's suicide as she hangs herself from the family's balcony. Anger, fear, and resentment create rumors that threaten to tear the family apart. The family has a small shop selling middle eastern goods and live together in an overcrowded flat. The old man BEHDAD chose exile for his family to escape religious persecution in Iran, but finds himself becoming an increasingly fanatical Muslim himself. Squashed into the 2 bedroom flat with BEHDAD are his son HAMID, his daughter FARUZEH and her husband ABBAS and their son HOSRO. Conflicts within the family arise from various factors—from the son who seeks sexual liaisons everywhere, from the son-in-law converting to Buddhism, to the grandson who no longer wants to go to Mosque with his grandfather, to the little stray dog the son brings home, which is initially completely rejected by the devout Muslim grandfather, only to be reinvented by him after he becomes attached to it. Around this growing relationship, his bonds with the other family members fray, nearly fracturing because of his own imposed bigotry and outside forces.

The following scenes show the relationship arc between BEHDAD and the dog.

SCENE 23
INT.--BABAI FLAT, CORRIDOR--DAY 1

HAMID kicks open the front door. He's carrying a dirty Jack Russell dog in his arms. BEHDAD comes to the sitting room doorway.

> BEHDAD
> What is this? Put it down and kick it out the door.

BEHDAD turns to go back in the sitting room. He looks over his shoulder at HAMID frowning.

> BEHDAD , Con't
> And wash your shoe seven times. Hands, jacket, all seven times!

HAMID kicks the door shut behind him.

BEHDAD turns round sharply back to HAMID and takes a step forward, pointing at him.

BEHDAD , Con't
You fool! Never touch a dog. Get it out of here!

HAMID shakes his head stepping away from BEHDAD.

HAMID
I can't, I've saved him! Some bastard left him tied to a lamp post outside the
shop.

BEHDAD
I don't care what some other bastard did! You're not having a dog. Oh no!
You tried as a boy and now you think I am old and gaga? Take it back where
you found it!

HAMID
I can't Dad, he won't do any harm.

BEHDAD
The Angel Gabriel won't enter a home with a dog inside!

HAMID
Angel Gabriel doesn't visit us, even if we don't have a dog!

BEHDAD
How do you know what the Angel Gabriel does?

BEHDAD takes a step forward and snaps his fingers in front of HAMID's eyes.

BEHDAD , Con't
What is all this rescuing dogs? What's wrong with your brains?

HAMID sighs.

HAMID
Listen, I took him to the Dogs Home, and they said if no one adopted him he'd
be put down.

HAMID shakes his head and smiles.

HAMID , Con't
So I had to save him! He's a great dog; he'll make a great pet.

BEHDAD
A pet?

BEHDAD slap himself on his forehead glaring at HAMID.

BEHDAD, Con't
You're not a bloody Kaffir, and what is this adoption rubbish? Nonsense!

BEHDAD jabs his finger pointing at HAMID.

                         BEHDAD, Con't
          Is he a human orphan? And no reason to keep a dog as a pet, it's a waste of
          time.

                         HAMID
          Why not? What's wrong with him? Look at him!

HAMID holds the dog out to BEHDAD who recoils backwards.

                         HAMID , Con't
          I've named him Turpin after the famous highwayman.

BEHDAD takes a quick glance at the dog, who's looking most sorrowful.

                         BEHDAD
          Listen Idiot! If I'm praying and that dog walks within a stone's throw of me,
          my prayer is made null and void.

TURPIN lets out a pitiful howl.

                         BEHDAD, Con't
          Muslims can't keep a dog, unless it's for guarding a farm or cattle.

                         HAMID
          That's it! We need a guard dog, rising crime in the area and all that, he'll be
          useful.

                         BEHDAD
          Don't talk rot! Look at him! A guard dog my arse! He's no bigger than a cat!

                         HAMID
          He'll grow! He's intelligent; he'll bark if robbers try and break in!

BEHDAD narrows his eyes, peering more closely at the dog.

                         BEHDAD
          Hmm; he has a black patch over his eye that's a bad sign! Black dogs are
          Satan's and must be killed!

HAMID chuckles.

                         HAMID
          Kill Scooby Doo? Kill Lassie?

                         BEHDAD
          Of course not!

BEHDAD throws up his arms, incredulous.

                    BEHDAD, Con't
        Are you blind? I've seen them on the telly; they're not black!

SCENE 24
INT.--BABAI FLAT, SITTING ROOM - NIGHT 1
FARUZEH, ABBAS and HOSRO are sitting round the table finishing dinner. The television
is on in the background.

FARUZEH, a pragmatic woman, is dressed in track suit bottoms, a sweat shirt and
sneakers. She has shoulder length hair tied in a pony tail.

ABBAS is a chubby man with bucked teeth. He embraces the Orient, wears Japanese Happi
coats decorated with bamboo and dragons and T-shirts with Chinese characters saying
'Good will.' and 'Long life.' Tonight, with BEHDAD out the way, he's wearing his favorite
clothes: A Japanese silk kimono, his Geta wooden Japanese flip flops on high wooden
blocks, and his frizzy hair drenched in oil is tied up in a samurai topknot.

HAMID is lying on the sofa. The dog is lying on HAMID's stomach watching his face with
raptured love. HAMID has a cushion on his head, shading his eyes from the glaring
chandelier lights.

                    HAMID
        Hosro, do me a favour and turn off the chandelier.

HOSRO gets up from the table and goes over to the light switch on the wall.

                    ABBAS
        Huh! When he said he'd ordered Cathedral lights, we had no idea.

As HOSRO sits down, ABBAS turns to him.

                    ABBAS , Con't
        And stop helping him shop on the internet, I ask you? Look at it!

                    HOSRO
        I told him it'll bring the ceiling down.

HAMID takes the cushion off his head and pushes it behind his neck. He sighs and smiles
dreamily, speaking slowly.

                    HAMID
        Our old man sits for hours every day under his chandelier, his old dry stick
        bones and leathered skin basking in the brilliant light like the sun. And he
        dreams how long ago he lived in a land far from these lead grey skies.

                              ABBAS
More like remembering his days as the school master caning all the students.

                              FARUZEH
That's not fair, you know he wasn't like that then, he was fun.

                              ABBAS
So you keep telling me.

                              FARUZEH
Well he was.

FARUZEH pushes her plate away.

                         FARUZEH, Con't
He changed after we came here and after mum….and I feel sorry for him.

                              ABBAS
Try feeling sorry for me. Where is he anyway?

                              FARUZEH
At the mosque.

                              ABBAS
I wish he'd bloody go and live there.

                              FARUZEH
HOSRO! Don't pick your pimples at the table.

                              ABBAS
He's always clearing his phlegm, belching, and farting.

                              HOSRO
I don't.

FARUZEH glares at HOSRO.

                              FARUZEH
Don't be smart!

ABBAS, oblivious to his son and wife, pushes his chair from the table and stands up,
stretching his arms.

                              ABBAS
Prayers every bloody morning. He's kicked a hole in the bedroom door.

                              HOSRO
He hasn't, it's just dented.

FARUZEH
HOSRO! Who asked you to butt in? Go and finish your homework!

HOSRO saunters out.

ABBAS strides round the room re enacting his hardships.

ABBAS
How many times have I trodden on his syringes in my bare feet? I ask you. I
sat on one too the other day. I got the needle stuck in my arse; it snapped,
and I had to go to Casualty.

ABBAS clutches his buttocks and treads gingerly in front of HAMID grinning at him.

ABBAS, Con't
Just think! I had to wait three hours because they said it wasn't an
emergency, and I couldn't even sit down.

FARUZEH is laughing at him. ABBAS' face glows red and shiny, and he stops grinning.

ABBAS , Con't
Stop laughing, I've had enough.

FARUZEH
Great, I'll go to the estate agents tomorrow, we'll move out.

ABBAS
Don't start again. We've got a house, remember? In bloody Wimbledon with a
sitting tenant who won't die.

FARUZEH
So? It was a great deal and she's past eighty.

ABBAS
Some people live to be a hundred.

FARUZEH
I'll rent us somewhere.

ABBAS
Yeah, do that! Money down the drain, and you know we'll have to take him
with us, so what's the point?

They both look over at HAMID on the sofa with the cushion behind his head. He waves at
them.

HAMID
Faruzeh's right! You need your own home, I've told you before, I'll take care
of Dad.

                              ABBAS
         Give us a cigarette.

HAMID comes over to the table and sits down. He offers his packet first to ABBAS and
then to FARUZEH. They sit together blowing smoke and saying nothing. ABBAS puts his
leftover dinner down on the floor.

                           ABBAS , Con't
         Here Turpin, come on boy!

The dog bounds over, his tail wagging and licks the plate clean.

                            FARUZEH
         Don't let Dad catch you!

FARUZEH turns to HAMID.

                         FARUZEH , Con't
         Didn't he tell you to take the dog back where you found him?

                             HAMID
         Can't remember, he said a lot of things. Do you want to stay here Turpin?

HAMID smiles nodding at the dog.

                          HAMID , Con't
         Yes, you do! Don't you?

SCENE 32
INT.--BABAI FLAT SITTING ROOM- DAY 2
HOSRO is sitting at the dining table eating breakfast, and the dog is sitting on the floor
next to his chair watching his every move. HOSRO throws him toast crusts, and the dog
stands up on his back legs and gobbles them up.

BEHDAD comes through the doorway.

                             BEHDAD
         Down, Turpin! Hosro, dog's saliva is dirty, so you can't let it lick you or get its
         wet fur on your clothes. The animal is a fool.

                             HOSRO
         Oh Baba, look at him, watch him catch this!

HOSRO tosses a crust in the air, and TURPIN leaps up and snaps it up.

                                BEHDAD
Better than a Hoover! But you know a little puppy once stopped an angel
from entering a house because it was unclean. It is wrong! This Turpin is a
rascal and a bad influence. We should send him to one of those dog homes.

TURPIN looks with his glowing soft brown eyes at the old man when he says this, as though
he understands perfectly, and he hangs his head.

                                HOSRO
Look Baba you're upsetting his feelings!

                                BEHDAD
Don't be ridiculous! No one listens to me in this house. How can a dog listen?
It has no brains.

BEHDAD stomps over to the armchair and sits down.

HOSRO gets up and takes his breakfast tray out to the kitchen, and the dog sits quietly
watching the old man who ignores him.

The letterbox clacks open and shut, and the dog races out the door to the hallway skidding
on the tiles.

TURPIN trots back into the sitting room with a newspaper in his jaws, and drops it on the
floor next to Behdad's chair.

                            BEHDAD , Con't
Tsk tsk, now you've defiled my newspaper with your saliva.

BEHDAD inspects the newspaper.

                            BEHDAD , Con't
Hmm just a bit damp.

BEHDAD looks at TURPIN.

                            BEHDAD , Con't
All right, all right, sit!

He waves his hand at TURPIN like a priest giving benediction.

SCENE 45
INT.--BABAI FLAT SITTING ROOM- DAY 3
It's late afternoon. BEHDAD is sitting under his thousand- watt chandelier basking in the
light.

TURPIN is sitting on the floor watching the prayer carpet; he slowly and delicately moves to
his feet and sits down on the soft carpet.

                                    BEHDAD
Don't you dare! That's my prayer carpet. Don't look at me like that, you've
been brought up badly and never learned to behave.

BEHDAD shakes his head, with a sardonic expression.

                                 BEHDAD, Con't
Nothing but a delinquent! Tsk tsk!

The dog runs out the room and returns with Behdad's slippers, dropping them down in
front of the chair.

                                 BEHDAD , Con't
Now you've contaminated these too!

BEHDAD ignores the dog and stares out the window at the muddy dirt grey sky while the
dog runs in and out the room amassing a pile of offerings around the old man: FARUZEH's
pink fluffy mules, an old newspaper, and a carpet brush. He watches BEHDAD, waiting,
and then he gently paws at his leg.

                                 BEHDAD , Con't
What's all this? Did I ask for this rubbish?

The dog holds out his little paw, and BEHDAD in a trance reaches out his hand and shakes
it solemnly. BEHDAD lets go of the dog's paw and looks at him.

                                 BEHDAD , Con't
Freezing cold feet! Those imbeciles don't know how to look after you! Do you
know Hosro would be dead by now if it weren't for my intervention on
numerous occasions?

BEHDAD shakes his head, watching the dog with a solemn stare.

                                 BEHDAD , Con't
And what a stupid name 'Turpin!' Who ever heard of a dog named after some
idiot highway robber? Now what we need is a name that suits; with the right
number it will bring you some luck.

BEHDAD gets up from the chair and hobbles over to the shelf. Fetching his calculator, pen
and paper he sits down at the table.

                                 BEHDAD , Con't
Asad or Behrang? Now!

BEHDAD turns and talks to the dog.

                                 BEHDAD , Con't
Every Arabic letter stands for a number, and we call this Abjad.

BEHDAD totals and subtracts, punching away on his calculator.

> BEHDAD , Con't
> Hmm, number one is not good for you! It's the sun number, and the rays of
> the sun will develop character such as arrogance and determination, very bad
> for a dog, I think.

The dog hangs his head.

> BEHDAD , Con't
> Don't take it to heart. I shall give you the perfect name.

BEHDAD quickly jots down some names.

> BEHDAD , Con't
> Peshman Babai? Parviz Babai? No! Bad numbers are two, six and eight!

BEHDAD looks at the dog.

> BEHDAD , Con't
> These are the people who are full of problems and unsuccessful.

BEHDAD taps away on the calculator.

> BEHDAD , Con't
> I have it, Cyrus! Yes it has the perfect number! Now follow me.

BEHDAD makes his way to the door with the dog following him.

SCENE 79
INT--BABAI FLAT SITTING ROOM - NIGHT 7
HOSRO and BEHDAD are sitting at the dining table looking at Internet web shops.

HAMID is standing leaning out the window smoking, his back facing the room.

> BEHDAD
> No, no, those won't do, tsk! Something more, well, higher off the floor and
> protected from drafts. Did you know his feet are always cold?

> HOSRO
> How could I know? How do you know?

> BEHDAD
> Don't be a smart arse! We all know he offers his paw to shake.

> HOSRO
> Yeah, he's so clever!

HOSRO chuckles slyly and points at BEHDAD.

                    HOSRO, Con't
          Baba, you shook his paw.

                    BEHDAD
          I might have done, just once, or twice.

BEHDAD looks away and peers through his spectacles at the computer screen.

                    BEHDAD , Con't
          Ahh! Now that's more like it, that one.

BEHDAD jabs his finger at the screen.

HOSRO leans forward to look, his head almost touching BEHDAD's.

                    HOSRO
          Are you sure Baba?

                    BEHDAD
          Yes, it's the best one! If you're going to do something, do it properly, that's
          what I say.

                    HOSRO
          Why can't he sleep on my bed?

                    BEHDAD
          He can't!... Next you'll have me buying him a four poster bed with silk sheets.

                    HOSRO
          They probably only sell them in America.

                    BEHDAD
          You never know, let's go and look.

HOSRO types in 'Luxury dog bed'.

SCENE 85
INT.--BEHDAD'S BEDROOM - DAY 8
HAMID appears at the doorway.

BEHDAD ignores HAMID; he is mechanically eating fudge sweets; now and then he tosses
one to the dog who is sitting on the end of his bed.

                    HAMID
          Dad you'll make the dog fat! He's beginning to look like a baby pig.

                              BEHDAD
                Shut up! What do you know? Here you are Cyrus.

BEHDAD tosses the dog another fudge cube.

SCENE 113
INT.--BABAI FLAT SITTING ROOM- DAY 8
It's late afternoon. BEHDAD is sitting in his chair wearing a long white grubby tunic, and
he's reading a newspaper.

CYRUS is asleep on the prayer mat.

HOSRO is studying his physics homework at the dining table.

                              HOSRO
                Baba, can I use your calculator?

                              BEHDAD
                Getting stuck? Huh! You have to learn to concentrate on numbers, see here!

BEHDAD strides on his bandy legs across to the book shelf, trying to walk low and stay
hidden, his legs bent, his back bent, his head hung down, he creeps along as though hiding
from snipers that only he can see.

                            BEHDAD , Con't
                Give me a number, any number! What's the root? Ha, I can tell you without a
                calculator.

BEHDAD gets a huge calculator down from the shelf and slides it across the table to
HOSRO, then he shifts stiffly back to his chair.

                            BEHDAD , Con't
                Now, if your names on the wrong number... Umm? You can make it into
                number five, and that'll cut off all these bad workings... and you'll get
                something someway.

                              HOSRO
                How?

HOSRO smiles at BEHDAD feigning interest since he already knows. He's heard the story a
hundred times before.

                              BEHDAD
                If your name is not agreed with you, you can have the name in number five. It
                will work for your prosperous. And, this is a very deep story, you have to
                watch when you change your name... You have to write it a hundred thousand
                times! Tsk!

BEHDAD shifts in his chair, holding onto the arm rests he settles back and looks out the window remembering.

> BEHDAD , Con't
> Now back at home we had a neighbor; she was a widow and only had one son, and he was a fine boy, you know? Very tall, very honest and hardworking. Then came the time for him to marry and his mother chose him a wife. All the astrology was perfect, PERFECT!

BEHDAD turns to face HOSRO shaking his head with a grimace.

> BEHDAD , Con't
> But it was no use at all, this girl... She was nasty to the mother, wasted her husband's money down the toilet on perfumes and jewellery, and would not keep house because she was divooneh... crazy!

BEHDAD taps the side of his head.

> BEHDAD, Con't
> All day at the cinema, no laundry, no cooking, nothing! So, of course, he divorced her! Then after a year he married again, and this time his mother gave much money to the astrologists to get it right. They looked for a wife who would be diligent in the kitchen and you know what?

HOSRO shakes his head, a slight grin on his face.

> HOSRO
> What?

> BEHDAD
> This girl burnt down the kitchen and argued like the devil with everyone. She had a sharp tongue, better she had been born a dumb mule, and so he divorced again.

BEHDAD shifts forward in his chair, his hands on his knees.

> BEHDAD , Con't
> Then at last I said to the widow, 'We must change your son's name, there is nothing else to be done.' So after much calculation he was named Hooman, I gave him some exercise books, and he wrote his new name a hundred thousand times. I told his mother, 'Now you must find a girl by the name of Kobra, no other name will do.' It was all in the numbers you see? And you know what?

HOSRO shrugs.

> HOSRO
> What?

BEHDAD slaps his thigh grinning.

                              BEHDAD
He married a fat beautiful girl named Kobra, and she was kind to his mother
and generous with beggars; most of all she gave him nine children! Think of
that, nine! Now nine is a very auspicious number, too...

The doorbell rings. BEHDAD gets up and shuffles out the doorway.

HOSRO hunches over his books. He can hear BEHDAD talking on the intercom in the
corridor.

                         BEHDAD , Con't
                          (OFF SCREEN)
         Why so late in the day? Well bring it in! At last!

HOSRO hears banging and the door being slammed shut, and then BEHDAD calling him.

                         BEHDAD , Con't
                     (OFF SCREEN TO HOSRO)
              The furniture has arrived!

A cellophane covered settee slides through the doorway, followed by BEHDAD pushing it
across the floor. HOSRO gets up and races to help carry the tiny settee across the sitting
room.

They rip off the plastic cover.

BEHDAD pushes the furniture around putting the settee next to his own armchair.

                         BEHDAD , Con't
              Now Cyrus! Come on! Up!

CYRUS jumps onto his own miniature faux black leather settee with leopard print
cushions.

                              HOSRO
              Look there's room for me too!

HOSRO sits down next to the dog, and BEHDAD plonks himself down in the armchair.

                              BEHDAD
Do you know I saw a film on the telly once, about an old rich woman who had
one of those sausage dogs. Guess what?

It slept in a four-poster bed with golden posts. Ridiculous woman, what a
fool! Hah hah!

HOSRO giggles.

                                HOSRO
Really Baba?

                                BEHDAD
I remember it had curtains for privacy.

HOSRO and BEHDAD laugh together. Suddenly the doorbell rings again.

                            BEHDAD , Con't
Tsk, what have those delivery fools forgotten now?

SCENE 121
EXT.--PARK BENCH--DAY 9
BEHDAD is sitting in a long tunic with his jacket pulled tightly about him, and CYRUS sits
at his feet on the dusty grass, his head on one side watching BEHDAD.

BEHDAD is staring ahead, his eyes narrowed, remembering.

                                BEHDAD
I gave him the best name! Our prophet said, 'Give your child a good name.'
and what did I do? I gave him the best! A name with number three... So is it
my fault?

BEHDAD smiles bitterly and looks down at the dog.

                            BEHDAD, Con't
He betrayed me once a long time ago. I forgave him, you know. He was just a
child. He couldn't help it, and I've never blamed him. It was my own fault.

BEHDAD sighs blowing air through his lips.

                            BEHDAD, Con't
I fear he follows after me. Yes, Cyrus, I have sinned, but that was a long time
ago. I've changed. I've paid my penance.

BEHDAD shakes his head.

                            BEHDAD, Con't
No, it cannot still be my fault! Everybody knows that some of these people
with good numbers like one, three and nine, still they are having problems!
And why?

BEHDAD looks down at the the dog.

                            BEHDAD, Con't
I'll tell you! Bad marriage combinations can ruin a man for life no matter
what his name.

CYRUS whines softly.

BEHDAD pats the dog's head and sighs deeply.

> BEHDAD , Con't
> You're right; he's not married. But since the fight... he's living with some Kafir woman! He thinks I don't know.

BEHDAD slaps his forehead.

> BEHDAD , Con't
> Of course! We must get him away from her. He needs to marry, and we have to find a Muslim girl with the right number.

BEHDAD stands up and stares ahead with determination.

> BEHDAD , Con't
> In the end all will come right! Maybe we will find one for Hosro too! Come along.

Shot from long distance:
BEHDAD slowly walks towards the blocks of flats on the other side of the park, his back bent and the dog at his heels. A lonely old man walking against the wind.

CYRUS sits down holding out his paw. After a few paces, BEHDAD turns back; he inspects the dogs paw and picks him up. BEHDAD continues walking slowly towards the flats carrying the dog in his arms.

SCENE 155
INT.--BABAI FLAT SITTING ROOM--DAY 12
BEHDAD, HAMID and HOSRO struggle across the room, keeping a hold of MUMMY AKBAR to bring her parallel to the sofa.

MR AKBAR, FATIMA, and HAFSA follow them into the sitting room.

BEHDAD gives out and lets go; he bends over the sofa armrest winded.

MUMMY AKBAR slips out of Hamid's grasp and with her legs still gripped around HOSRO's thighs her head drops with a thud on the floor.

HAMID staggers back and lands sitting on a chair.

> MR AKBAR
> Careful now, nice and easy does it.

> FATIMA
> Mummy?

HAFSA has her arm around FATIMA.

HOSRO is stooped over MUMMY AKBAR still holding her legs. He heaves them on the sofa and steps away.

MUMMY AKBAR is lying twisted on the floor with her legs up on the sofa.

BEHDAD straightens up, panting, out of breath. He rallies to the situation.

> BEHDAD
> That's right, well done, Hosro! Legs up, head down, perfect position for a fainting fit... A cushion for her head!

HOSRO turns away and scurries out the sitting room. BEHDAD looks at the Akbars.

> BEHDAD , Con't
> Not to worry... to overcome a faint... the legs must be kept above the head to increase the flow of blood to the brain.

BEHDAD grabs a cushion and pulls MUMMY AKBAR's head up by her headscarf and shoves the cushion underneath. He nods reassuringly at the Akbars.

HAMID lights a cigarette.

> BEHDAD , Con't
> She'll come round in no time at all!

> FATIMA
> Mummy?

HAFSA is still hugging FATIMA to her.

> HAFSA
> Uncle, don't you think we should call an ambulance?

MR AKBAR looks down on MUMMY AKBAR in bewilderment. He sneaks a look at the table laden with dishes, and shakes his head firmly.

> MR AKBAR
> No ambulance. Give her time to come round naturally.

> BEHDAD
> Exactly! Not a scratch on her; she'll wake up soon enough... Well Hussein, shall we eat?

HOSRO enters with a large dish of Baklava. He moves the dishes around on the table to make space.

                              MR AKBAR
          Lots of delicious food sitting there waiting for us, come along Fatima, Hafsa,
          take your seats.

          What?

MR AKBAR smiles coldly at HAFSA.

The Akbars take their places and sit down to eat. HAMID strolls over to the table.

HOSRO creeps towards the door.

BEHDAD sees HOSRO making his escape and calls him.

                              BEHDAD
          HOSRO, come and eat!

HOSRO sits down.

Everyone starts to eat in silence except BEHDAD, who chews with his mouth open and
makes loud sucking sounds.

MUMMY AKBAR reaches her arm in the air as though waving.

CYRUS sniffs around MUMMY AKBAR. He begins to lick up the caster sugar stuck to her
lipstick and chin.

HAFSA notices CYRUS licking MUMMY AKBAR's face. She cries out.

                              HAFSA
          The dog is licking Auntie's face!

                              BEHDAD
          No mind. He's well trained!

BEHDAD claps his hands.

                              BEHDAD, Con't
          Here Cyrus, come boy and sit.

The dog trots back to the table and sits next to BEHDAD's chair.

MR AKBAR doesn't pay any attention as he greedily devours his food.

MUMMY AKBAR makes kicking movements, pawing with her feet like she's pedaling a
bicycle and then she lies still.

                              MR AKBAR
          Your son-in-law not coming to eat?

                    BEHDAD
Can't, he's got a weak stomach!

                    MR AKBAR
And your daughter?

                    BEHDAD
Tsk! She must attend to him.

BEHDAD nods his head slowly as though meditating the fact.

                    MR AKBAR
In fact, I thought he looked very pasty.

BEHDAD tosses a couple of meatballs on the floor for the dog.

FATIMA is looking at HOSRO. She's winding her ringlet round and round her finger and giving him coy looks from across the table.

CYRUS, on the floor next to Behdad's chair, is devouring the tiny fried meatballs.

BEHDAD notices HAFSA looking at him sourly. He nods to her.

                    BEHDAD
No need to disapprove, not at all! This dog is not a pet but a guard dog. Recently there have been a lot of houses broken into, even in the middle of the night.

                    MR AKBAR
Dogs should be kept outside, even guard dogs.

                    BEHDAD
How? We live in a flat!

                    HAFSA
I think it's too small to be a guard dog, don't you Uncle?

MR AKBAR ignores her and keeps on eating.

                    BEHDAD
Maybe he is small, but never judge by the size! He also barks every time someone passes by in the hall. Now that's useful as a warning isn't it?

                    HAFSA
I should think it must be very annoying. I expect in a block of flats like this he must be barking on and off all day.

                    BEHDAD
Well, maybe he is, and maybe he isn't.

                              MR AKBAR
                    Hafsa, please do not argue this issue!

MR AKBAR turns to BEHDAD.

                              MR AKBAR, Con't
                    A woman needs a husband, or she'll start to bicker and think she's equal to a
                    man!

MR AKBAR takes a piece of Baklava.

                              MR AKBAR, Con't
                    Ahh! This is delicious, I must compliment your daughter's cooking!

                              BEHDAD
                    A family recipe, my wife, hers were... tsk... more clover! Faruzeh now... hmm,
                    just so-so... Now tell me about your plans, I too have been considering
                    opening a new business, maybe some laundry service or this pizza delivery
                    franchise.

HOSRO is staring at his plate, ignoring FATIMA.

FATIMA is now winding ringlets round her fingers on both sides of her head. She stops
and glares at HOSRO.

                              FATIMA
                    I want to go home!

                              MR AKBAR
                    What! What's this?

                              FATIMA
                    I want to go home and NOW!

                              MR AKBAR
                    Nonsense! Shut up and mind your manners.

MR AKBAR turns back to his plate and carries on eating. FATIMA looks angrily at HOSRO.

                              FATIMA
                    He made a rude face at me, and he did this.

FATIMA holds up her hands, curling her left hand into a tunnel, she feverishly pumps her
right index finger in and out the hole mimicking sexual intercourse.

BEHDAD jumps up and lands a heavy clout round HOSRO's head. HAMID stands up.

                              HAMID
          Dad, leave him alone, I don't believe he did that!

Hosro rubs his head.

                              HOSRO
          I didn't.

MR AKBAR stands up.

                              MR AKBAR
          Are you calling my daughter a liar?

                              HAMID
          She's just mistaken that's all.

                              HAFSA
          She might be lying; she's done it before. Don't forget Uncle, Fatima, and the
          Kebab boy; she made that up!

MR AKBAR barks at HAFSA.

                              MR AKBAR
          Shut your mouth!

MR AKBAR leans into HOSRO's face.

                              MR AKBAR, Con't
          Did you or did you not make that disgusting sign to my daughter?

As MR AKBAR says 'disgusting,' he sprays some spit on HOSRO's face.

HOSRO jumps up.

                              HOSRO
          I feel sick!

HOSRO wipes his face and stumbles out the room.

HAFSA is chewing down the Baklava like a rabbit.

FATIMA sits sulking with her arms crossed.

HAMID, MR AKBAR, and the old man are still standing.

                              MR AKBAR
          Well, I never!

MR AKBAR kicks back his chair; it falls. He hollers at the girls.

MR AKBAR, Con't
Fatima, Hafsa. Thank Mr Babai for such a wonderful lunch. We're leaving!

HAFSA
What about Auntie?

They all turn to look at MUMMY AKBAR forgotten on the floor; she hasn't moved.

MR AKBAR takes a jug of water from the table and goes over to her.

MR AKBAR
Maimuna?

MR AKBAR stares down at MUMMY AKBAR, prodding her with his foot.

MR AKBAR, Con't
MAIMUNA, ENOUGH!

MUMMY AKBAR doesn't move, but her eyelids flicker.

MR AKBAR pours water down on her face from his standing position. It splashes, heavily streaking her face with blotches of make up that run down her cheeks.

HAFSA
Uncle, I think you'd better call an ambulance!

MR AKBAR
Very well, if I must!

Unconvinced, MR AKBAR turns to HAMID.

MR AKBAR, Con't
Where's the telephone?

HAMID
In the hall.

SCENE 161
INT.--BABAI FLAT BEHDAD'S BEDROOM--DAY 13
BEHDAD is sitting in bed reading a newspaper and eating sweets from a tin. His hand goes from tin to mouth to tin, tossing sweets in his mouth and chewing fast.

The dog is sitting on HAMID's bed.

HAMID is emptying a chest of drawers, putting piles of ironed clothes into his suitcase.

BEHDAD ignores HAMID as though he weren't there. HAMID closes the case and straightens up.

                            HAMID
Dad? I'm off now, I'll drop in after work on Monday...Dad, I'm off!

                            BEHDAD
You're not OFF! Do not speak to me as though you are just going out and will
be home later! I know you are living with that Patty woman! You've left your
home and never had the guts to say so!

                            HAMID
Dad, that's not fair.

HAMID looks guilty.

                          HAMID, Con't
Look, would you like me to sleep here tonight?

                            BEHDAD
Don't bother. I don't need your pity!

                            HAMID
Anyway, you gave my bed to Turpin weeks ago and don't deny it, Dad. Look at
him!

                            BEHDAD
Don't talk rubbish. He's just a guard dog. I need him in the room at night.
Dogs alert their owners to gas leaks, fires, and heart attacks.

                            HAMID
You didn't have to give him my bed. He could sleep on the floor!

                            BEHDAD
I haven't given him your bed, nonsense!

                            HAMID
Then why's my bed got a black and white Dalmatian blanket with Cruella de
Vil?... Anyway, Cruella used dogs to make fur coats; it'll give poor Turpin
nightmares.

                            BEHDAD
His name is Cyrus! Hosro chose the blanket, nothing to do with me, and who
is this Cruella?

                            HAMID
She's a villain in a dog film, ask Hosro.

                            BEHDAD
Just get on with your packing. Leave if you must, but you're not taking Cyrus
with you.

                                HAMID
      I don't want him.

                                BEHDAD
      He's the only one who listens to me, just think of that! I have a family, but the
      only one I can talk to is a dog, and he's not even permitted!

BEHDAD goes back to reading his newspaper.

                                HAMID
      I'll be in after work...every day, same as usual I promise.

HAMID softens his voice.

                                HAMID, Con't
      Look Dad, why don't you get a hobby?

                                BEHAD
      Hobby my arse!...Hobbies are for idiots who've nothing better to do! Out of
      here and take your suitcase with you!

BEHDAD turns his back on HAMID, rolling over and upsetting the sweets on the bed.

HAMID picks them up and puts them back on the bedside table.

HAMID leaves the room, returning a moment later with a gigantic canary yellow ghetto
blaster, with a red ribbon tied in a bow on the handle.

                                HAMID
      Dad, look, I've bought you a present.

BEHDAD still has his back to HAMID.

                                BEHDAD
      Don't want a bloody present. I'm not a child, I'm not bloody gaga yet!

                                HAMID
      You don't know what it is!

HAMID presses play and a muezzin call starts.

BEHDAD turns round sitting up. HAMID stops the cassette.

                                HAMID, Con't
      It's a proper cassette player not CD, and I bought you a brand new tape, too!

                                BEHDAD
      It's enormous, and it's bright yellow, bloody ridiculous!

                                    HAMID
I can take it back and get you a smaller one.

                                    BEHDAD
I don't want you wasting time running backwards and forwards to the shops.
I suppose I'll get used to it. How many decibels?

                                    HAMID
A lot, it's the loudest they had in the store!

                                    BEHDAD
Put it under my bed, before that buffoon Abbas gets sight of it!

BEHDAD lies back down.

                                BEHDAD, Con't
I'm running low on sweets. Faruzeh put me on rations. Bring me some tins of
Okho Chi next time!

                                    HAMID
OK, I'll see you on Monday.

                                    BEHDAD
Wait! This Patty, she must change her name.

                                    HAMID
What?

                                    BEHDAD
Yes, it'll bring you both some luck, enough just to change a little.. Patsil!
That'll work for you. Now remember, okay?

                                    HAMID
Thanks Dad, Patsil it is.

HAMID smiles and pats BEHDAD on the shoulder and then pats the dog. HAMID picks up
his suitcase and leaves quietly closing the door behind him.

When the door shuts Behdad sits back up. He looks at the dog sitting on Hamid's bed.

                                    BEHDAD
Cyrus, you see what an ungrateful son I have? You were abandoned by your
master and I by my son! We both know what it is to nurse a viper in our
bosom!

SCENES END

Fall Splendor

Karen Colstrom

Clink Our Glasses

Bill Connolly

I've not even taken a sip of this idea
but I'm already woozy with the reality
that you are 21 years old.
I still pause when I refer to something
I did thirty years ago
but that still falls short
of this shocking celebration.

But this is your day,
and so damn my aging disposition
and the same to your hesitance
to raise your glass and celebrate you.
Don't leave your elbow on the table
and tilt the glass a little,
smirking self-consciously.
Hoist that thing high and proud and...

Now what do I say at this precious moment,
that formal silence between hoist and sip?
What words fit this milestone,
this occasion of "finally!" for you
and "oh my!" for me?

Some dram of wisdom
about "with privilege, comes responsibility"?
Perhaps something with a splash of humor,
about how you can't have wine...and whine?
Or maybe just a refreshing remembrance
of when you loved your sippy cup?

Yes, the occasion is special
but the words that come to mind
will not be unique, witty, or profound.
Simply that I love you,
am proud of you,
and cannot believe
that the girl is woman,
the kid is adult...
but I'm still just Dad.
Always.

Writing in Bed

Bill Connolly

This is where we are, dear.
The clock glares green numbers at me,
familiar ones.
Most normal people are asleep,
and the bed is warm with you and flannel sheets.
I hold a portable light just inches from my notebook,
hopelessly writing against the night,
hoping for the generation of something for us.
No, not "that novel" you speak of
with a casual certainty that makes my neck hot.
Just some words in a not-so-special book
with a cheap Bic pen
to tell me not necessarily that I will "make it"
but simply that I should make this.
That the decision to forfeit what is now
five minutes of sleep is one I will value,
even if just tomorrow.
The house is quiet with slow breathing
and the whirr of the furnace.
The windows are tight against the muffled sounds
of suburban, winter night.
There is death outside
and even in the edges of my soul,
but as my legs sink deeper and deeper
into the mattress
and I pass sad judgment on another day
of unfulfilled promise,
I feel alive and hopeful.
Because of this.
Because of you.

Lake, Trees, Sky

Roberta I. Mayes

DIRT LANGUAGE

—A dramatic premonition in six pop-up scenes

Willy Conley

SCENE 1
> Present. A shady, pop-up floral shop in an urban area. A WORKER is re-potting some plants.
>
> Note: Lines identified as "speaking" indicate that the character mouths the words without actually speaking; the words should be subtitled. The purpose for this is to offer more roles to Deaf actors as well as add another layer of spectacle. All other lines of dialogue are in sign language with subtitles.

CUSTOMER 1

(enters; "speaking")
I'm looking for some basil. Do you have any?

> (WORKER gestures being deaf and not able to hear.)

CUSTOMER 1

("speaking")
Oh, I am so sorry.

> (Takes out a smartphone, types a message, and shows it to WORKER. WORKER nods head and gestures "wait." WORKER gets a basil plant off a shelf and gestures "$10." CUSTOMER 1 pays for the herb and waves goodbye. WORKER goes back to re-potting.)

CUSTOMER 2

(enters; surreptitiously signs)
Excuse me. I'm looking for some tomato plants.

WORKER

What kind would you like? I have Grape, Cherry, Big Boy.

CUSTOMER 2

Big Boy, please.

> (WORKER locates a Big Boy plant, takes a flash drive from a pants pocket, and stealthily inserts it into the dirt of the tomato plant.)

WORKER

Here you go. $5, please.

CUSTOMER 2
(pays, nods, and exits.)

BLACKOUT.

SCENE 2
Two government agents stand behind a tripod with an SLR camera with a long
telephoto lens on it. They take turns looking through it. One of them snaps photos
while the other makes notes on a clipboard. Both speak unintelligibly to one
another, but it is obvious that they are discussing what is being witnessed through
the camera's viewfinder.

BLACKOUT.

SCENE 3
An outdoor zone fenced off with barbed wire. There is a sign posted with a large, red
banned symbol overlapping a pair of hands. A GUARD with a rifle stands beside it.
Some Deaf PRISONERS–looking cold, hurt, and hungry–move about slowly within
the zone. One of them has no hands; the ends of the prisoner's arms are nubs with
dirty bandages wrapped around them.

PRISONER 1

(secretly)
You know when they'll let us back inside?

PRISONER 2
(horrified)
Are you crazy?? Don't sign! You know what happens if.... They want all prisoners outside for eight
hou—

GUARD

("speaking")
NO FUCKING SIGNING, YOU SHITHEADS! ABSOLUTELY NO FUCKING SIGNING!!
UNDERSTAND??? YOU GODDAMN SHIT-FOR-BRAINS!

BLACKOUT.

SCENE 4
Same pop-up floral shop and worker as in SCENE 1., except in a different location or
shop arrangement. WORKER is potting some new flowers and secretly inserting
flash drives into the soil of each pot. Deaf CUSTOMER 3 enters.

CUSTOMER 3
(discreetly)

Tomato. Big Boy, please.

(WORKER nods and quickly brings forth the plant. Gestures $5. Receives payment. CUSTOMER 3 exits.)

BLACKOUT.

SCENE 5

Government office with a projection screen and projector. An SLR camera with a telephoto on a tripod is in the background. Some AGENTS are seated around a table with a potted tomato plant on it. On screen is a photo of WORKER selling a potted plant to a customer.

GOVERNMENT AGENT

("speaking"; holds up a flash drive)
We caught another deaf fuckin' asshole! Disguised as a pop-up florist.

(Another slide is projected with a close-up of a flash drive being pushed into the soil of a potted tomato plant.)

The sons-of-bitches are spreading the fuckin' sign language on videos in these flash drives. Here's what one of them looks like.

(A video of a Deaf person teaching some rudimentary sign language plays on the screen.)

This filthy, fuckin' language must be banished all over our country! Understand?

(All nod.)

BLACKOUT.

SCENE 6

A pop-up fruit stand. Boxes of fresh green and red apples, oranges, and bananas can be seen. WORKER 2 is polishing the apples.

CUSTOMER 4

(enters; "speaking")
I would like to get 2 apples, please.

(Worker gestures being deaf and unable to hear. The customer points to the apples and holds up the "2" handshape. Worker nods and puts two apples in a small paper bag; gestures $1. CUSTOMER 4 pays and leaves.)

CUSTOMER 5

(enters; signs small and quickly)
One apple.

WORKER 2

Which kind? McIntosh, Granny Smith, or Red Delicious?

CUSTOMER 5
Red Delicious.

(WORKER 2 puts one apple in a paper bag, and gestures half of $1. CUSTOMER 5 pays, grabs the bag, nods, and exits.)

(WORKER 2 goes to the side of the stand to grab some more apples to refill the display box. On one of the Red Delicious apples, WORKER 2 carves out a piece, inserts another small flash drive, re-inserts the apple piece over it, and sets the apple with the others on display.)

The End.

Tree Reaching Over Dam Into Lake

Roberta I. Mayes

I Fly Again

David Blumenfeld

I once became a bird, black-winged
sleek-feathered, fast-flying, air rider.
I didn't mean to, didn't want to, didn't
expect to, didn't consider it *imaginable*.
I'm a rational type, you see, no nonsense
no bull, no mystical flights-of-fancy, no
craziness, no LSD-induced hallucinations
feet on the ground *always*, just science and
common sense and when science and common
sense conflict, then science, science and science only
no God, no faith, no illusions, nothing to lead reason astray

... ever.

Until

Paul took me to a swamp high on a dune in the Oakland Hills
cattails everywhere, wind blowing swiftly, sand in the air
bright sun and the smell of swamp water, pungent, acrid
with excrescences of minnows, tadpoles, large gray-brown
toads huddled at the marsh's edge, snakes --- green, yellow and
orange tongue-flickers --- a hard-shelled tortoise blinking, staring
placidly, implacably at me, a clicking croaking chorus of frogs
and waterfowl, when suddenly overhead
they appeared ---
a hundred of them; no, a thousand, it seemed, blazing, blasting
in unison across the sky, a single black being, black unity of
black parts moving as one against a blue background, dipping
swooping, rising again, whirring deafeningly, my head spinning
to the drumming of their powerful black wings, their sharp beaks
clacking and, without warning, the great whirring thing
of a thousand parts down-rushed within an inch of my head
taking me up into it, sucked-up, absorbed, unified, merged
human no longer, and flock-fused I flew, flew for a furious
fleeting instant...or an eternity...no me, no them, one
bird-being, avian essence, inexpressible
even in poetry.

Then, as suddenly as they had come, they were gone.
I was my old self --- human, mundane, rational.
Now life proceeds as it once did:
normal, prosaic, humdrum.

(stanza break)

But occasionally at night
when sleep overtakes me
the birds return and, in a dream,
I lose my myself and
I fly again.

I'm Beautiful

Aline J. Awada

"I'm...beautiful,"
I muttered to myself
as I stared back at my reflection in the mirror.
I observed my
fried, pin-straight highlighted hair,
my chipped red nails,
my face,
caked with makeup,
my tight crop top,
and exposed cleavage.
And I wondered if there ever truly was a day
when the girl in the mirror was content
with who she is.
If there ever was a day
when she didn't question her worth.
If there ever was a day
she didn't desire
to change something about herself.
There was always more I could do:
more makeup to try,
more clothes to buy.
more boys for whom to cry.
Day by day,
social media and society's expectations
polluted and corrupted my mind,
and the aura of the nerdy,
curly-haired Arab girl
faded away.
And day by day.
I'm showered with compliments--
from people telling me
I look infinitely better than I did before.
Finally, I fit into the beauty standard.
I feel seen, respected, and desired,
making me truly believe
that with this disguise,
I'm beautiful.

Bolinas Lagoon, Low Tide

Linda Enders

Contributors' Notes

Cid Andrenelli began writing in Sri Lanka, while filming fly on the wall documentaries in remote villages. Some of her stories have been published by Rambutan literary and Easlit. In Italy, she began writing theatre plays, most recently in 2023 'Il Caso Olivo' aka 'The Wife Chopper' has been performed in several theatres in Florence with more venues later this year. *God Damn Dog* is her first screen play. In her own words: I love writing, you can make people love each other, kill each other, betray or redeem themselves, it's like playing God. She has a blog https://cidandrenelli.wordpress.com/ Her email is: bedandbreakfasthanoi@gmail.com.

Aline J. Awada is a Lebanese and Brazilian 16-year-old living in Brazil. During the pandemic, she moved to Lebanon, a couple of weeks after the August 6th explosion. She spent weeks feeling isolated in a completely new environment while simultaneously undergoing puberty and transformative physical and hormonal development. This drastic change had a significant impact on many aspects of her life, including her relationship with her self-image and body, family, and home country. As she struggled to determine her identity, she found peace in the vulnerability of telling her story and uncovering her feelings through writing poems in her journal.

Alex Barr's full-length plays have been performed on the London fringe and at the Edinburgh Festival, toured in Wales, and broadcast on BBC radio. His short plays include 'Touching the Tree', performed by Sherman Theatr Cymru and published in *Bare Fiction* magazine, and 'Oh Coronado' performed by Bee Line Theatre Company at the Cockpit Theatre, London. Alex Barr's recent short fiction is in *Tears in the Fence, The Lampeter Review, The Interpreter's House, New Welsh Reader*, and *The Last Line Journal*, and at mironline.org, litromagazine.com, feedlitmag.com, reflex.press, and samyuktafiction.in. His short fiction collection 'My Life With Eva' is published by Parthian.

Mark Blickley grew up within walking distance of New York's Bronx Zoo and is a proud member of the Dramatists Guild and PEN American Center. He is the recipient of a MacArthur Foundation Scholarship Award for Drama and an M.F.A. in Playwriting from Brooklyn College. Blickley is the author of the story collection *Sacred Misfits* (Red Hen Press, Los Angeles). His multi-genre collaborations with artist Amy Bassin include *Weathered Reports: Trump Surrogate Quotes from the Underground* (Moira Books, Chicago) and the text-based art book *Dream Streams* (Clare Songbirds Publishing House, New York). His latest book is the flash fiction collection *Hunger Pains* (Buttonhook Press).

David Blumenfeld (a.k.a. Dean Flowerfield) is an emeritus philosophy professor and associate dean who in retirement returned to writing stories, poetry, and children's literature, which he abandoned in his thirties to devote full-time to philosophy. One of his recent pieces was cited in *Best American Essays, 2022* as a "notable essay;" another received a Pushcart Prize nomination; a third was "highly commended" in the 2022 *Autumn Voices* international poetry competition and has just been republished in *Five Points*. His work for children has appeared in *The Caterpillar, Balloons Lit. Journal, Smarty Pants, Dirigible Balloon,* and various anthologies. Davidcblumenfeld.com

Stacey Bowerman lives in the Missouri Ozarks surrounded by exquisite nature and diverse circles of friends. Her education concentrated on women's studies and creative writing. Her educational and life experiences provide a challenging, thoughtful, and questioning personal outlook. In the early 2000s, she left school to focus on the necessity of treating her schizophrenia. She now lives a slower paced life without the demands of a formal career or education. She enjoys creative and critical writing. She also devotes time to researching various intriguing and often random topics. She lives with her emotional support dog, Juno. She can be reached at staceyannbowerman@gmail.com.

Steve Brisendine–writer, poet, occasional artist, recovering journalist–lives and works in Mission, Kansas. His most recent collections are *Salt Holds No Secret But This* (Spartan Press, 2022) and *To Dance with Cassiopeia and Die* (Alien Buddha Press, 2022), a "collaboration" with his former pen name of Stephen Clay Dearborn. His work has appeared in *Modern Haiku, Flint Hills Review, Connecticut River Review* and other journals and anthologies. Write to him at steve.brisendine@live.com.

William Robert Carey wrote and directed, "Jesus In Cowboy Boots," inspired by his novel of the same name. His play about a parent and transgender child, DANIEL/DANIELLE, won the 2019 Scribe Play Competition Award. A monologue from it was published by Smith & Kraus in "WE/US Monologues for THE GENDER MINORITY." He is also the author of IDOL MINDS, (produced by Stages/OC), FAIRY TALE (Sundog Theatre, NY), and SHE CAME BACK (T. Schreiber Studio, NY). His memoir, "How NOT To Make A Movie: An Independent Filmmaker In Hollywood Hell" was published by McFarland Books and his short story, PEGEEN'S PUNISHMENT, by "Cerasus Magazine." http://williamrobertcarey.com/

Mark Clarke is a photographer based in northeast Kansas. His most significant artistic influences are his experiences with local and international travel, his fondness for abstract and impressionist art, his love of nature, and a genuine desire to share with others. He especially values making a connection with the natural world and strives to communicate its beauty through his photographs.

Karen Colstrom currently lives in Osage County on the family farm. Native-born in Kansas, her photography has been inspired by this rural setting close to the Flint Hills. Karen's artworks are currently on display at the Emporia Art Center's, "Glaser Art & Gift Shop," which is located in Emporia, Kansas. To view more of her photography visit: prairiedesignphotography.com.

Willy Conley's most recent book is *Photographic Memories–Essays, Playlets, & Stories*. His other books are: *Plays of Our Own–An Anthology of Scripts by Deaf and Hard-of-Hearing Writers, Visual-Gestural Communication: A Workbook in Nonverbal Expression and Reception, The World of White Water–Poems, Listening Through the Bone–Collected Poems, The Deaf Heart–A Novel, Vignettes of the Deaf Character and Other Plays*, and *Broken Spokes*. Born profoundly deaf, Conley is a retired professor and chairperson of Theatre Arts at Gallaudet University (the world's only liberal arts university for deaf and hard-of-hearing students) in Washington, D.C.

Bill Connolly is a recently retired New Jersey educator who has been changed by his loves and losses, inspired by his teachers and students, and humbled by the poets he has read and heard. His poetry has appeared in *Philadelphia Stories*, *The New Jersey English Journal*, and publications of the National Writing Project. Every three years, he writes poems for his two children's birthdays; "Clink Our Glasses" is one of his favorites for his daughter.

Brian Daldorph teaches at the University of Kansas and Douglas County Jail. His most recent publication is *Words Is a Powerful Thing: Twenty Years of Teaching Creative Writing at Douglas County Jail* (University of Kansas P, 2021).

Suzanna C. de Baca is a native Iowan, proud Latina, publisher, author and artist who is passionate about exploring change, transformation and life in and beyond the Heartland. She is an inaugural member of the Iowa Writers Collaborative and her poetry been published or will soon appear in: Choeofpleirn Press' *Glacial Hills Review, Etched Onyx Magazine; Impermanent Earth; iō Literary Journal; Voices de la Luna; Wholeness: A Wising Up Anthology; Written Tales,* and other outlets. She lives in the small rural town of Huxley, Iowa.

Linda Enders uses her iPhone camera to focus attention on moments and tiny details as she was taught by Oregon writer, Kim Stafford.

Andy Graber is a self-taught artist who was born and raised in the northeast part of the United States. He currently calls the beautiful state of Nevada his home. Besides creating various forms of artwork, Andy also has strong interests in writing and music.

Peter J. Grady has volunteered with the Marshalltown Community Theatre since 2003 as an actor, director, and currently, as a board member. Grady coordinates the Theatre's annual playwriting competition for Iowa writers (information available by writing to mctplayfest@yahoo.com). He authored and performs a one-man show, "Unconditional Surrender: A Visit with Ulysses S. Grant" (see https://petegrady.wixsite.com/ulysses-s-grant). Grady graduated from St. Ambrose College in Davenport, Iowa and the University of Iowa College of Law. He authored this play in reaction to Dobbs v. Jackson Women's Health Organization, 597 U.S. ___ (2022), which quashed the constitutional right of women to control their own bodies.

John Grey is an Australian poet, US resident, recently published in *Sheepshead Review, Stand, Washington Square Review* and *Floyd County Moonshine*. Latest books, *Covert, Memory Outside The Head* and *Guest Of Myself* are available through Amazon. Work upcoming in the *McNeese Review, Santa Fe Literary Review* and *Open Ceilings*.

Patricia L. Hamilton is a Professor of English in Jackson, Tennessee, and is the author of *The Distance to Nightfall*. She won the Rash Award in Poetry in 2015 and 2017 and has received three Pushcart nominations. Her most recent work has appeared in *Slant, The Ekphrastic Review, Plainsongs, Prime Number Magazine,* and *Innisfree Poetry Journal*.

Susan Hansell's complete plays are cataloged at <www.susan-hansell.net> and at <https://newplayexchange.org/users/5806/susan-hansell> (where *Who Will Witness for the Witness* is reviewed) or at <https://www.dramatistsguild.com/members/susanhansell>. The St. Louis Actors' Studio presented the world premiere of *Who Will Witness for the Witness* at the Gaslight Theater's LaBute New Play Festival, July 8-31, 2022. *Who Will Witness for the Witness* serves as the first act, with the one-act play *Every Concentrated Fragment* as the second act, along with a devised third act, to comprise the new three-act play, *At Dawn with the Rain and the Stars*.

Rosalie Hendon (she/her) is an environmental planner living in Columbus, Ohio. Her work is published in *Change Seven, Pollux, Willawaw, Write Launch,* and *Sad Girls Club,* among others. Rosalie is inspired by ecology, relationships, and stories passed down through generations.

Arnold Johnston lives in Kalamazoo and South Haven, Michigan. His poetry, fiction, non-fiction, and translations have appeared widely in literary journals and anthologies. His plays, and others written in collaboration with his wife, Deborah Ann Percy, have won over 300 productions and readings, as well as numerous awards and publications across the country and internationally; and they've written, co-written, edited, or translated over twenty books, their most recent being *The Old Fart Plays*, forthcoming from Dramatic Publishing Company. Arnie's latest projects are *The Infernal Now* (poetry, Kelsay Books, 2022); *Where We're Going, Where We've Been*, (poetry, FutureCycle Press, 2020); *Swept Away* (novel, Atmosphere Press, 2021), and *Mr. Robert Monkey Returns to New York* (a collaboration with Debby, Brandylane Publishers, 2021). He was chairman of the English Department (1997-2007) and taught for many years at Western Michigan University, where he co-founded the creative writing program and founded the playwriting program. He is now a full-time writer. <Johnston-Percy-Writers.com>

Roberta I. Mayes, a practicing Wiccan, is drawn to nature, so she willingly spends as much time as she can outdoors. She is quite often barefoot as she takes photos because she's happiest with her feet touching the earth or dangling in a cool stream.

Michael Moreth is a recovering Chicagoan living in the rural, micropolitan City of Sterling, the Paris of Northwest Illinois.

Launched on an unsuspecting commercial world, **Margaret Pearce** ended up copywriting in an advertising department. She took to writing instead of drink when raising children. She completed an Arts Degree at Monash University as mature age student. She has had articles, poetry, short stories, and mainly teenage novels currently listed on Amazon, Kindle, and writers-exchange.com.

Jennifer M. Phillips is a bi-national poet, a retired Episcopal Priest and AIDS Chaplain, gardener, grower of Bonsai, painter, and has been writing and publishing poetry and prose since age seven. Phillips grew up in upstate New York and has lived in Britain, New England, New Mexico, St. Louis, Rhode Island, & Cape Cod, Massachusetts. Her work has won several awards and appeared in over eighty journals. Her two chapbooks are *Sitting Safe in the Theatre of Electricity* (iblurb.com, 2020) and *A Song of Ascents* (Orchard Street Press 2022). A poem is like a little brass pan to carry fire's coals through the winter, and so she writes.

Marge Piercy has published 20 poetry collections, most recently, *On the Way Out, Turn Off the Light* [Knopf]; 17 novels including *Sex Wars*. PM Press reissued *Vida, Dance the Eagle to Sleep*; they brought out short stories *The Cost of Lunch, etc.*, and *My Body, My Life* [essays, poems]. She has read at over 575 venues here and abroad.

Judith Present is an actress, playwright and director whose theatre company PRESENTARTS brings historical characters to the stage for historical societies, museums, and organizations for fundraisers. She is also a fine art digital photographer and enjoys merging the two in performances. Judith's short stories have appeared in several literary magazines throughout the country. Her photographs have also appeared in magazines. Ms. Present's websites: theater-site: Presentarts.org, photo-site: judithpresent.zenfolio.com.

Kait Quinn (she/her) was born with salt in her wounds. She flushes the sting of living by writing poetry. She is the author of four poetry collections, and her work appears in *Reed Magazine*, *Watershed Review*, *Chestnut Review*, and elsewhere. She received first place in the 2022 John Calvin Rezmerski Memorial Grand Prize. Kait is an Editorial Associate at Yellow Arrow Publishing and a poetry reader for *Black Fox Literary Magazine*. She enjoys repetition, coffee shops, tattoos, and vegan breakfasts. Kait lives in Minneapolis with her partner, their regal cat, and their very polite Aussie mix. Find her at kaitquinn.com.

S.M. Stevens began writing fiction during back-to-back health crises: a shattered pelvis and ovarian cancer. She writes contemporary novels, but drama is her first love. Her *Bit Players* series of Young Adult novels is set in a high school drama club. She worked in the Theatre Department at Cornell University, and in the University of Southern Maine's drama department, while earning an English degree. The characters in *The Wallace House of Pain* are also the leads in her forthcoming novel *Beautiful and Terrible Things* (Black Rose Writing, 2024). www.AuthorSMStevens.com.

Gerald Uyeno makes his living as an engineer: writing science fiction and creating graphic images of the future. He also enjoys creating visual artwork with pencil, pen, or computer, and in the past several years, he has taken a keen interest in photography as an art form.

Buff Whitman-Bradley's poems have appeared in numerous print and online journals. He podcasts at thirdactpoems.podbean.com His most recent books are *At the Driveway Guitar Sale*

(Main Street Rag), *The Heron Could Be Lost* (Finishing Line Press), And *What Will We Sing?* (Kelsay Books). With his wife, Cynthia, he lives in northern California.

Mark Clarke Photos
Fb/Ig @MarkClarkePhotos
markclarkephotos@gmail.com

Submit your stories!
TO THE HUDSON REVIEW
2023 SHORT STORY CONTEST
FIRST PRIZE: $1000
SECOND & THIRD PRIZES: $500
10,000 WORD LIMIT. NO SUBMISSION FEE.
OPEN TO FIRST-TIME CONTRIBUTORS.
SUBMIT ONLINE AT WWW.HUDSONREVIEW.COM/SUBMISSIONS
September 1–November 30

Winner of the 2022
Kenneth Johnston Nonfiction Book Award

Available as an ebook from Choeofpleirn Press.
Print books available wherever books are sold.

Jonathan Holden Poetry Chapbook Contest

2023 Winner and Finalist

Choeofpleirn Press

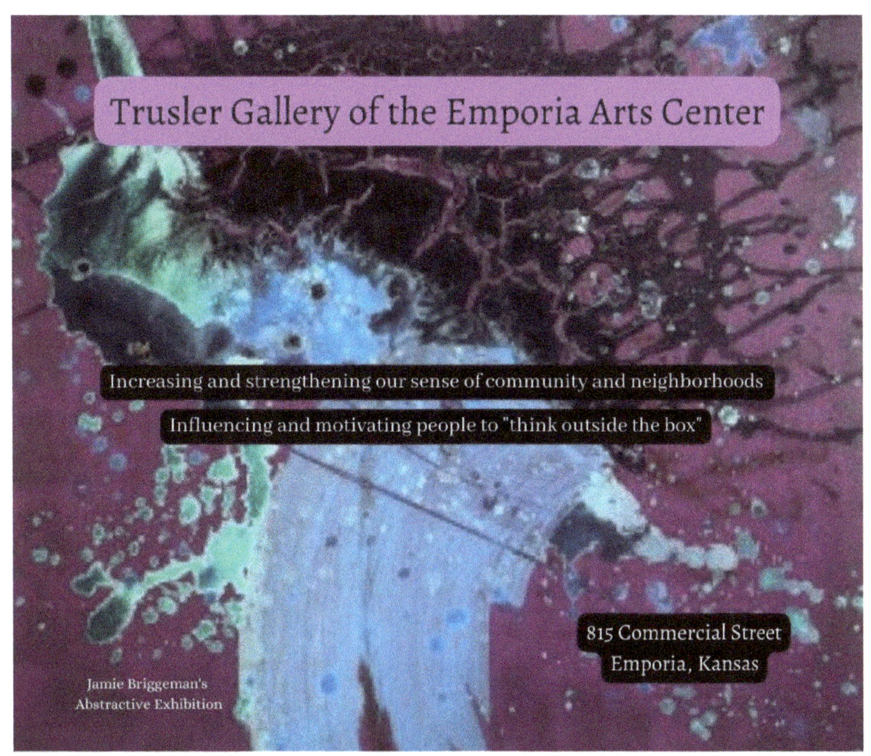

Trusler Gallery of the Emporia Arts Center
Increasing and strengthening our sense of community and neighborhoods
Influencing and motivating people to "think outside the box"
815 Commercial Street
Emporia, Kansas
Jamie Briggeman's
Abstractive Exhibition

Thank you for supporting our press!
Fun Fact
Choeofpleirn
pronounced "chuf-plern"
is a combination of our
surnames by alternating
the letters
www.choeofpleirnpress.com

Listening for Low Tide

Available at Amazon and
Choeofpleirn Press

Too much happens at ground level:
the kids selling candy or delivering
newspapers shortcut through the yard,
the neighbors' dogs blare their alarms
in unison, and teens, shielded by the heartbeat
of their music, speed down the street.

Two stories above the ground.
I welcome the afternoon sunlight
as it stretches across the rug,
my cat moving with it. From the opposite
window, the shadows cast by trees
overspread the ground, the sunlight only
hitting the treetops. Sound waves lap
against the building, the tide at its lowest
each night when the owl in the park
starts to hoot its presence.

Drama is one of theoldest forms of literary arts, dating back
further than writing itself.

An outstanding compilation of one-act plays, short screenplays,
an excerpt of one full length screenplay, poetry, and art, this issue
of *Rushing Thru the Dark* leads us through the perils and pitfalls
of being human. It also demonstrates the human capacity for love
and tolerance of differences. Choeofpleirn Press is delighted to
present works by the following contributors:

Cid Andrenelli	Peter J. Grady
Aline J. Awada	John Grey
Alex Barr	Patricia L. Hamilton
Mark Blickley	Susan Hansell
David Blumenfeld	Rosalie Hendon
Stacey Bowerman	Arnold Johnston
Steve Brisendine	Roberta I. Mayes
William Robert Carey	Michael Moreth
Mark Clarke	Margaret Pearce
Karen Colstrom	Jennifer M. Phillips
Willy Conley	Marge Piercy
Bill Connolly	Judith Present
Brian Daldorph	Kait Quinn
Suzanna C. de Baca	S.M. Stevens
Linda Enders	Gerald Uyeno
Andy Graber	Buff Whitman-Bradley